EXPECT!

EXPECT!

Put the pills down and drain the tub...
I'll tell you how you can make it better.

Banjo Martini

iUniverse, Inc.
Bloomington

EXPECT!

iUniverse books may be ordered through booksellers or by contacting:

iUniverse
1663 Liberty Drive
Bloomington, IN 47403
www.iuniverse.com
1-800-Authors (1-800-288-4677)

Because of the dynamic nature of the Internet, any web addresses or links contained in this book may have changed since publication and may no longer be valid. The views expressed in this work are solely those of the author and do not necessarily reflect the views of the publisher, and the publisher hereby disclaims any responsibility for them.

Any people depicted in stock imagery provided by Thinkstock are models, and such images are being used for illustrative purposes only.

Certain stock imagery © Thinkstock.

ISBN: 978-1-4620-6008-5 (sc)
ISBN: 978-1-4620-6009-2 (e)

Printed in the United States of America

iUniverse rev. date: 10/19/2011

Special thanks to:

~ Daddy, thank you so much for giving me the heart to care for others more than myself. I know you didn't always understand me, but thank you for loving me unconditionally and for loving everyone that I loved. I miss you every day that I live.

~ Mom, thank you for supporting everything that I've ever done. Some things didn't work out, most things did. The love that we share is the most important thing in the world to me. I can't wait to sit next to you during the next full moon.

~ Lisa, you'll never know how much you mean to me. You are my bucket carrier and I'm so thankful for you. I love you "Long as I Live".

~ Tomas, thank you for being such a wonderful companion. Thank you for your forgiveness, thank you for letting me be part of your children's lives, and thank you for loving me.

~ To my true friends, whether or not you made the pages of this book, I wouldn't be alive today if it weren't for you. Thank you. You saved me. That's what I hope to pass along.

~ Strangers, thank you for reading this book. It is my greatest wish that the words within touch you and inspire you to make a difference in the world and eliminate hatred and increase the power of love.

~ Jayne Kelly, thank you for your amazing passion for music. With every word that was written, the sounds of your keyboard were there to inspire me. Don't ever stop tickling those ivories. Nobody does it better…

~ To my beloved friends who didn't find the support they needed, I'm fighting for you!

Table of Contents

- Prelude 1
- Chapter One: Fear 3
- Chapter Two: Change. .9
- Chapter Three: Self Realization. 26
- Chapter Four: Courage. 35
- Chapter Five: Strength .47
- Chapter Six: Friendship 62
- Chapter Seven: Confusion 81
- Chapter Eight: Excitement 85
- Chapter Nine: Bewilderment 98
- Chapter Ten: Love 103
- Chapter Eleven: Bliss .109
- Chapter Twelve: Surprise 118
- Chapter Thirteen: Disappointment. 123
- Chapter Fourteen: Sacrifice. 131
- Chapter Fifteen: To Settle 137
- Interlude. 145
- Chapter Sixteen: Acceptance. 149
- Chapter Seventeen: Expect 151
- Chapter Eighteen: Do the Right Thing. 155
- Chapter Nineteen: Do Unto Others 158
- Chapter Twenty: Be Different...Be You 161
- Chapter Twenty-One: Beat the Bully 163
- Postlude 166

~ Prelude ~

Expect was written just for you. It isn't intended to be a guideline for your life. It's first intent is to show the young people of the world that life is worth living. It is the journey of one gay man, who at a few points in his life, thought about ending it. With faith and perseverance, he remained alive to tell you a story about how great your life can be if you don't give up.

The second intention of this journey is to let parents, siblings, friends, classmates and perfect strangers know what gay people, both young and old, are holding onto within their hearts and minds.

There are people all around you every day that are facing their own difficult battles. Be kind to them no matter how they treat you. Eventually the seed of kindness that you planted in their mind will sprout and they will be thankful for the smile that you sent their way.

This is simply the story of how a forty-two year old man made it through the tough times and landed in an unexpected happy place…just because he didn't give up.

For now, just put the pills down, drain the tub and take a few minutes to read about what to EXPECT...

Chapter One

"Fear"

(To consider or expect with alarm)

There is an emotion that lives within all of us that is referred to as fear. Like love, it is instilled in our very essence from the moment of conception. This very powerful force is permitted to grow within us right next to the opposing force of love. It is love's great misfortune that fear is fed and allowed to grow and overshadow the goodness of love, while the nature of giving and caring are knocked down and beaten to be referred to as 'weak' or 'sissy'.

No matter how strong the love of your parents is for you, the more of the world that you are exposed to, the more you become aware of fear: The first time you see the light of the world, you are spanked to make you cry; the first time you try to crawl, you feel the pain of a hard surface against your tender skin; the first time you try to walk, you feel the power the coffee table has over

3

your chin and the first time you fall in love you are bewildered by the fact that the object of your desire has fallen for a member of the opposite sex: A reality that is as foreign to you as driving a sharp blade through your own heart.

It is then that you realize there is something different about you - the moment when love hides behind the omnipresent fear. It is when you feel the loneliest and the most afraid.

~ When I was being brought up in a small town in North Carolina, it was common for all of the neighborhood kids to go outside and play until dinner and then gather at the home of whoever's mom had prepared dinner that night and then go back outside to play until the street lights flickered on as the first of night was taking over the warmth of the day.

We played the usual games of Cowboys and Indians, we rode bikes and played hide-and-go-seek. Most of us boys had motor bikes which we would ride through one of the neighbor's cow pasture and see who could sling the most cow patties on whoever was the unfortunate one to be bringing up the rear of the two-wheeler race.

Most of us were Baptist. Some of us (myself included) were deacon's kids and some of the other kids were known as PK's (Preacher's Kids). PK's were usually the worst in the lot as they had the strictest rules and therefore knew better than anyone else how best to break those rules. Some of the other kids were Presbyterian but we were allowed to play with them anyway, even though their parents drank beer. Alcohol in any form was considered a sin punishable by eternity in a burning lake of fire if you were brought up in a Baptist home.

Sleepovers were rare in our home, but on certain occasions I was allowed to have a friend over to stay the entire night which was a very special treat.

In those days the *Dukes of Hazard* was the program of choice on television and I had known for sometime that I had *unusual* feelings for one of the characters on that show. Most of my friends couldn't seem to stop talking about the female character, 'Daisy', while I couldn't stop thinking about 'Bo'. I even searched for hours for a poster that featured 'Daisy', because that wouldn't seem odd to have hanging on my wall, but this poster also had to feature a shirtless 'Bo'. Even with the threats of scalding skin, I couldn't suppress the feelings I had for him.

It was a hot summer night and my friend Thad was staying overnight with me. We did all the normal things that young boys do: we watched television, we played board games and we even talked about girls. But when it was time for bed, it was obvious that that night was not to be the usual sleepover. Something extraordinary was about to happen.

Instead of crawling into our individual bunk beds, we both decided to spread a blanket on the floor and sleep there instead. After having our last drink of water for the night, Thad and I crawled onto the red cotton blanket that had been on my bed for so long that it had faded to a soft pink. We talked for what seemed like hours about mindless subjects such as "Which is better? Mello Yello or Mountain Dew?" We kidded each other jovially about developing 'man hair' and we wrestled each other as our half naked bodies flopped clumsily around on each other. Finally, the conversation changed to the picture hanging on the wall: my shirtless Bo. Thad and I began discussing Bo's hair and how we would love to have hair just like his. Then we talked about his arms. They were perfect arms, indeed. We discussed how perfect his biceps were and how it was amazing how he had that vein running down the middle of his bicep that we strived to have some day. We also couldn't leave out his perfect chest; how it had just the right amount of hair and how perfectly formed his pectoral muscles were. The more we talked about Bo, the warmer the moonlit room became.

It was time to turn the lights out. After I got up and switched the little lamp off that was sitting on my desk, the room began to change to a warm glow as the bright July moon began to shine through the open window. I took my place on the floor right next to Thad and it seemed like I could no longer breathe. The thought of him lying so close to me wearing nothing but his tiny whiteys was almost more than I could bear. He must have been sharing the same feelings. Almost simultaneously we rolled towards each other wearing nothing but our stark white Fruit of the Loom briefs. As soon as our flesh touched, we both paused and pretended to sleep.

Terrified of rejection, I decided that it would be best to pretend that I had fallen asleep and sounded out a couple of fake snores. Shortly after I had fired off a couple of nasal flares, I felt Thad's hand creep to a place where only mine had been before. It was if I had waited my entire life for that very moment. We both trembled with fear but realized that we had gone too far to turn back. The following moments were intense as Thad and I rubbed each other and floundered around on the pink blanket. Our bodies grew wet with sweat and a gentle summer breeze just barely caused the curtains to rustle. The final rapturous moment came quickly and we collapsed next to each other. Before we went to sleep, Thad leaned over with his salty, sweet lips and gently kissed me good-night. No other words were spoken.

After we woke the next morning we acted as if nothing had happened the night before. We put our shorts and polo shirts on that we had worn the day before and headed down to the kitchen towards the smell of bacon where my mom had breakfast waiting for us. My father and sister were waiting for us at the table and I was terrified that there was some tell-tale sign that would offer up the story of last night.

I'm not sure what Thad was thinking as we sat down to eat but all I could hold in my mind was the thought of how I wished every night could be like the last and how I wished I could have every breakfast, for the rest of my life, sitting next to Thad and holding his hand without shame.

Suddenly, the name of Jesus was called as my father began to bless the food. At that moment Thad and I both trembled in fear as we thought of that lake of fire. ~

The feeling of fear and self-hatred are unfortunately still considered 'normal' in gay adolescents. Many are shamed into living a life of lies and deception in order to maintain social status, political gain or familial acceptance. Others simply can't withstand the pressure and don't make it through to fulfill the purpose of the life that they were put on this earth to fulfill.

If you are a gay person struggling with the fear of coming out, you need to know that you were created to be a blessing, just as you are. You are not a 'freak' and you were placed on this earth at this very special time to make a difference in the world around you. You were given a heart that is unlike any other and God trusted you with it because he knows you are strong and can be a blessing to everyone else around you.

You are unique; a special gift to earth. The next few years of your life could possibly be quite challenging and even frightening. Eventually you will find your way in the world. You will possibly need to change all of the friends that you have and you may need to change your environment entirely. Keep moving forward and eventually you will find happiness and forgiveness. You will even find acceptance. You can make it through and be a very happy person if you keep fighting and know what to expect. You can undoubtedly EXPECT…

Chapter Two
"Change"

———ഇ ——

(To Become Different)

The graduation from middle school to high school can be a very exciting time for most children. It can also be a very stressful and challenging time. It is at this crossroads of time when kids become aware of peer pressure and social status and begin to realize that the people who were their friends just a short while ago, have moved on in other directions and found different friends, discovered different activities and have begun to have romantic encounters with other people.

To a lot of adolescents this can be a very difficult time. Especially to one who has just realized that they are simply not interested in the same things that their friends are: Their friends have changed...and so have they.

When someone realizes they are 'different' from everyone else around them, it can instill a sense of self-doubt and a fear of not being accepted by their peers. A supportive environment is crucial at this stage of a person's life as it is the beginning of the developmental process of adulthood. It is the precise moment when a person begins to search for a place to belong, and without a positive influence and guidance, it is the time when a life can begin to spiral downwards towards a very lonely and dark place. There is always a place for one to belong. Something is always waiting to accept a person in search of company and self-acceptance. These open arms can be either good or bad.

The first years of high school can be difficult for anyone, but especially challenging for someone who is just realizing that they are gay and thus, different, and the world around them sees them as a freak or sick. There is a constant fear of danger and judgment. It seems that around every corner lurks the jock that wants to beat you up, or the kid that doesn't fit in anywhere else and finds solace in terrorizing you in front of others by calling you names and mocking you in hopes of making himself look cool.

To overcome a fear like this and accept the changes in others around you can be a very tiring experience, but the realization that everyone else around you is struggling to fit in as well can be extremely enlightening. It is important to realize that a person who bullies you is simply another lost soul in search of acceptance and is only preying on you because he or she is struggling with self-esteem issues just like you are. Friends that turn away from you are struggling with the same issues and were never really your friend to begin with. Some people in this life are placed in your life for specific reasons. Some are there to be a friend for life and others are simply there to occupy your time while you discover your mission on this great earth.

It is important to realize that with change comes possibility, and with possibility comes inevitability. Something must happen alongside change and it is up to you whether or not change can be good or bad.

Whatever stage of life you are in, it will inevitably change at some point. People will always be around you and influencing you in one way or another. Always know that even though your friends have changed…so have you.

⁓ The schools in the town where I grew up started high school in the eighth grade. Things had already begun to change drastically for me during the summer prior to my graduation from middle school to high school. My family and I moved to a different part of town and away from the neighborhood that I had always known. All of the friends that I had always played with were now moving in different directions. The one that bothered me most was Thad. He had discovered that it was not going to suit him well to be seen as different. The world of sports seemed to be his way out of the challenge of searching for his place to belong. And I knew nothing about sports.

The first day I ran into Thad in the hallway at school I was elated. I just couldn't wait to hear what all he had been up to over the summer and to learn from him how great things were going to be in high school. (Thad was a year older than me and already had a year in high school behind him so I knew he would be my perfect guide.)

When I walked up to Thad I expected to be greeted with that familiar smile that I had not so long ago fallen in love with. Instead, I was alarmed by his coldness and eagerness to shrug me away. What had happened? What had I done? I just couldn't believe that he wasn't as happy to see me as I was to see him. As he turned and walked towards his new friends, greeting them with high fives and barbaric shouts translatable only by a caveman, I felt myself become empty and afraid. I knew that I was on my own in this new and frightening world.

The rest of my first day in this brand new world was full of questions and doubts: Would I be able to make any new friends? How am I supposed to get through this without the love of my life beside me? Where would I fit in? Where I was to fit in was certainly not to be in the new class that I was forced to take. Gym was not my forte!

Later that night after I had sat through dinner with my family, I sat in my room and wondered what I could do to find the wonderful life that I was sure was eager to welcome me. It was then that I found my answer: I would develop a sense of style that was sure to make everyone want to be my friend. I would wear the most amazing outfits and polish my look to perfection.

I enlisted the help of my older sister for this transformation as she was sure to know what people in high school were drawn to. After all, she had four years of high school experience under her belt and I just knew that she could lead me in the direction that I should go.

Very willingly, my sister came to my rescue. That night she picked out an outfit that was sure to knock the socks off of everyone at school the next day.

The morning was full of excitement as I put on my Calvin Klein jeans, green polo cashmere sweater, pale yellow Tommy Hilfiger blazer and Tony Lama snakeskin boots. The final step to my transformation was grooming, so I met my sister in the bathroom where she was already armed with a hair dryer, a comb, and enough styling mousse to style a wooly mammoth.

When I first walked through the lobby at school that morning with my poofed up do and stylish wardrobe ensemble, I was shocked by my reception. I might as well have had a poster stuck to me that said, "Yes, I am a big flaming queer!". People began to snicker and point and whisper to each other as I passed by them. This was not at all what I had in mind. The thoughts of becoming the popular guy that everyone wanted to be near began to diminish as my head gradually sunk towards the ground and I made my way to my first class and hid behind my books.

Clearly, the preppy cowboy look was not going to render my salvation so I spent the next few days in search of a style that would work and finally something happened.

Marching band, chorus and drama seemed to be the worlds that welcomed me. The people in those classes all seemed to be as unique as me so I jumped in with both feet. The clothes that I wore were completely appropriate to these new people and before I knew it, people were actually copying my style! Finally…a place to belong.

The happiest times for me were in my artistic world with my new creative friends but I still had to venture out into the halls of 'normality high' and that was often very daunting for me. Especially considering the fact that there was one guy that just seemed to want to kill me.

Gary was from a part of town that I had never really been through. I had heard frightening tales about it, but had never known for sure what was down the streets of the area referred to by my friends as 'The Track'.

Gary was black and I had never been exposed to that culture before. Growing up, we were never around 'people of color' and that world was completely foreign to me. Everyone in our neighborhood was white, everyone in our church was white and all of my parents friends were white and, unfortunately, it was common for me to hear black people being referred to as 'niggers'. Not knowing anything about Gary or his life, I already had placed judgment on an entire culture simply based on his individual behavior.

Every time I ran into Gary in the hall, I broke out into a cold sweat and tried my best to hide so that he wouldn't see me because every time he did see me, he would call me things like sissy or fucking queer and faggot. He would often get right in my face and act as if he was going to punch me. It was as if I had somehow done something to this total stranger and angered him to the point of wanting to put a knife through my stomach.

Somehow, I managed to escape bodily harm from Gary, but there was a constant fear inside of me every time I walked down the halls of my school. Fear was constantly alive inside of me and fear is what led me to live the next few years of my life as a lie.

With the disappointing knowledge that I could never be accepted as who I was, I began to reach out into the world of romance by flirting with girls.

There were a lot of girls I could choose from but if I was going to take this route, I had to make sure that I chose the right one. She had to be able to suit my parents vision of what was perfect for me which meant she had to come from a 'good' family and she had to attend church. That seemed to be all of the prerequisites that my parents would assume, but I had different ideas. For me, she had to be beautiful and above all else…she had to be popular. That would surely guarantee popularity and acceptance for me.

My family had long since left the Baptist church and had become involved in somewhat of a movement. We were now attending an interdenominational church and I was deeply involved in the music programs of the church and because of that, I was often asked to sing solos.

One Sunday morning as I was singing my anthem of praise, I noticed a beautiful young girl from school smiling at me with a smile that was more than just a friendly hello.

Ashley would be the perfect girl for me I thought. She was beautiful and charming. Her hair was sandy blonde and bouncy. Every time she turned her head, her hair seemed to follow her like ripples in a calm lake. Her eyes were pool-water blue and they got brighter every time she smiled. She attended the same church that we did and she was one year younger than me and went to my school. The most important thing about Ashley was that she was a cheerleader… my in!

Ashley and I began dating innocently enough. We would go to the movies, to the mall and out to eat on a regular basis. I became very close to her family and would often just go to her house to hang out with them. Ashley also had an older brother that was also very popular in school and as much as I tried, I could not help but fantasize about him every time I was near him. He was everything I wanted to be. He was incredibly handsome, one of the most popular guys in school and he was a partier.

Being involved so deeply in the church forbade me to indulge in the activities of all of the other kids in school and I soon realized that was part of what was holding me back.

Ashley and I began to attend parties that the other kids were going to and I soon found myself being able to numb my old self by drinking a few beers just to fit in. Ashley and I began having a few beers in public to show the others that we were cool. We didn't get drunk, so that seemed to make it alright.

Ashley was the first girl that I had sex with. And I was her first as well. It was during a party at a friend's house, and after several beers. With the presence of an empty bedroom, we slipped in and clumsily removed each other's clothes.

Ashley was wearing a pretty sun dress that I had helped her pick out the week before the party. It was sleeveless and the soft silky dress that was light pink and green with a floral print slipped off effortlessly. After I removed my black t-shirt and jeans, I laid myself on top of her and we began to kiss each other frantically. The moment was just before happening and we were both breathless. As I put my hand inside of her bra and felt her breasts, all I could think was, "This has got to be done…and I am the one that has to do it."

Her naked body wasn't the kind of body that I so desired, but it was warm and alive. While the room was spinning around me it became clear what went where and we finally put the pieces together.

The actual act itself was less than magical, but I remember gaining a sense of power. Not over her, but power over myself. Within the first few seconds of feeling myself inside of her, a feeling of ecstasy rushed through me. The thoughts that were rushing through my head were, "I've done it! I've overcome homosexuality! I'm no longer the freak that some say I am!"

When the final thrust was over, we laid quietly there in each other's arms. Her words spoke of our undying love for each other and I tried to feel the same but the only thing I could think of was how I had been delivered from the burden of being a queer.

The following few months were filled with as much sex as we could possibly find time or place for. The feeling of newness began to diminish as well as our feelings of love for each other. And we began to see other people.

With encouragement from family, friends and certainly church, I had been taking private voice lessons in a nearby city from a well respected voice coach. This opened up a different world for me.

There were several students in Mrs. Winston's studio and one of the female students and I found ourselves gravitating towards each other.

Kirsten was a beautiful blonde haired girl with the voice of an angel. Her voice made me want to sit and listen to her for hours. She lived in the same town where we were taking voice lessons and her family was incredibly kind to me. We became very close friends and spent a lot of time together singing and laughing.

There was an occasion that Kirsten and I were to sing together and I was to spend the night at her house. It was a very exciting night for me as I felt that I had found a place that not only welcomed me, but also intrigued me.

It wasn't until the moments when I went into Kirsten's older brother's room to change my clothes when I discovered why I was so intrigued by this place: As I looked around her brother's room, I began to sense that something was different. There was unusual art work on the walls, everything was right where it should be, and there were only pictures of other guys on the dresser.

Immediately upon discovering that Kirsten's brother was gay, I began to re-examine myself and ask myself many questions: "Could it be possible that Kirsten's family knows about this? Could it be possible that they accept it? Why do I want her brother to come in right now and take me in his arms? Did I not win the battle over homosexuality?"

When I was ready to exit the room, I found myself wanting to stay there. In that moment, in that temple. Seemingly, someone had found rest within themselves and I wanted it to be me.

A few weeks later I was to be with Kirsten and her family again. This time to sing at her sister's wedding reception. It was to be an extraordinary event and there would be a bar. It was mine and Kirsten's plan to leave immediately after the reception and drive back to my parents house where we would spend the night and wake up the next morning and sing at my church.

The soirée was well underway and Kirsten and I had performed our song and were now to have dinner. The bar was very inviting to me so I approached it with enthusiasm and ordered my first glass of wine. At the age of sixteen, it seemed like a very mature thing to do so I visited the bar several times before my knees began to feel numb. Before I knew it, I was drunk. Kirsten finally took a place between the bar and my staggering body and informed me that it was time to leave. She also said that we had to say good-bye to her parents without them knowing that I had been drinking.

Somehow, I managed to put on a convincing act and the parental unit only assumed that I had really enjoyed myself at the evenings festivities. Kirsten took me by the hand and led me out to my car and informed me that she would be driving back to my parents house and that I had to stay awake and direct her on how to accomplish the task.

The drive back home that night seemed to be the shortest it had ever been. There was a smile plastered across my face and the two of us couldn't stop laughing.

There was an awkwardness as we entered my parents home. The laughter stopped and Kirsten and I stood face to face, now with a more serious countenance upon our young faces. Recognizing the look, I moved in closer to her and brushed her flowing blonde hair with my hand and leaned in and kissed her gently on her lips. The kiss was short and sweet but we both knew that our relationship would somehow be different from that moment on. After the kiss, I led her to the bedroom that she would be staying in for the night, kissed her once more, and closed the door behind me as I headed towards my own accommodations.

As I was lying in my bed that night, with my head still swimming from the wine, I found myself feeling extremely confused. I wondered why I had kissed her and I wondered what our friendship would evolve into after that night was over.

The next morning at church was a morning that I will never forget. With a throbbing headache from what I assumed was my first hangover, the new realization that I was still attracted to guys and the absolute guilt of being drunk the night before, Kirsten and I began to sing. The song was a song performed by Larnell Harris and Sandi Patti. The song was *I've Just Seen Jesus*, and it was a very emotion evoking and powerful song

Two measures into our duet, I began to cry. Not just any ordinary cry, but all out sobbing. As Kirsten continued to sing, I continued to weep. While I was falling to my knees from guilt and pleading for God's forgiveness, other church members began to gather around me, lay hands on me, and pray for my deliverance. After that I swore to be the best heterosexual Christian that the church had ever seen.

The next few months would prove to be some of the most trying of my life up until then. High school can seem like a prison to most kids, and that was what it was starting to feel like to me. Those years can be especially tough for someone who is having difficulty figuring out just what their essence is and how to cope with it. At that time, I didn't feel like I had anywhere to turn to where I could openly discuss my feelings and attraction to other boys. Everything I heard told me it was wrong, and everything I felt and thought told me it was the only thing that was right for me.

The jocks in the school, as well as some of the other misfits, began to notice that something was very different about me. Even though they had no idea of my inner thoughts and questions, they went by my mannerisms and began to tease me and call me names. They would see me coming down the halls of school and begin to walk like an exaggerated girl and laugh as I tried to change everything about my demeanor. Even though I had a wonderful group of friends, I still couldn't find the courage within myself to bring the topic of homosexuality up and hear their thoughts or judgments on the subject. Fear of losing every friend I had and being ostracized from the community kept me from being able to love who I was and show other people that I was of no threat to them.

Several months had gone by and Kirsten was now enrolled in the North Carolina School of the Arts and invited me to come and spend the weekend with her.

Thinking that the new surroundings would be refreshing from the misery that I was hiding within me, I decided to go. It had been a while since I had left her hanging in front of a congregation of complete strangers and I was curious as to how she would react to my arrival into her new life.

The morning finally came and there was a feeling inside of me that I couldn't figure out. An eagerness to get to Kirsten's school overwhelmed me and questions kept popping up inside my head like frogs trying to find escape from a bucket that was just a little taller than the reach of their leap. As I sped down the highway in my white Pontiac Grand Am, I wondered why I was so impatient to get there. After I rolled the sunroof back and pressed the gas pedal a little harder, I put in a Whitney Houston CD and allowed the sunshine to warm the top of my head and prayed for the whirling Spring air to wash the doubts out of my mind and release me into freedom and happiness. Whitney's version of *I Will Always Love You* was blaring out of my speeding white mode of transportation, and I sang along with a smile on my face and eagerness in my heart all the way to the school's main entrance.

As I drove through the gates to the campus I was overtaken by a sense of familiarity. The people who were walking around the campus all seemed so happy and energetic. It was a different world than the one I lived in and I immediately wanted to be a part of it. The people in this new world seemed to have their own individual styles and they acted like they didn't care about anyone else's…except for mine. Being the preppy guy on the campus didn't seem to be the normal sightings of their daily lives.

After I got out of my car and closed the door, it took a few moments for anyone to approach me. Finally a nice girl wearing what seemed to be a hemp sack, with dreadlocks, walked up to me and asked if I was lost. After informing her that I had been invited there by one of their own, she was more than willing to help me and pointed me in the direction in which I could find my friend.

A short walk was all that was involved to find Kirsten standing on the lush green grass, underneath a towering magnolia tree with her long blonde hair glistening from the shadows of the giant tree. She was now smiling and running towards me with her arms open wide to receive me.

The rest of the day was spent roaming the campus as she was telling me how exciting everything was there and how wonderful the people were. Her voice classes seemed to be her favorite and she couldn't stop talking about all of her wonderful new friends.

That night there was going to be a party and Kirsten asked me if I would like to go. Without hesitation, I screamed, "Yes! Of course!" I couldn't wait to be in the heart of this fascinating place.

The gathering was at one of the student's apartment and I saw things I had never seen before and smelled fragrances that had never before entered my nostrils. There were people smoking pot, there were drugs that I couldn't identify, and there were same-sex couples holding hands and kissing right in front of everyone. This both shocked and excited me.

Kirsten and I went into the kitchen and she grabbed us each a beer and we popped them open and began to mingle with the crowd. The people there enchanted me and I wanted to get to know each and every one of them.

Later in the night I found myself sitting in a circle with a lot of people I had never met before but were very interesting and seemed to be laughing at the most ridiculous things. But it was the guy sitting next to me that piqued my interest the most.

Mark was an extremely handsome black man and he seemed very eager to be near me. He was wearing cut off jeans and a white tank-top. His hair was black and curly and he had arms that looked like he had been lifting weights since he first came out of the womb. He asked if I would like to take a hit off of his joint and I told him that I had never done that before. Mark laughed and asked me to join him on the terrace if I would like to smoke with him.

Kirsten had fallen victim to one of the more chatty attendees and couldn't tear herself away from her. With little hesitation, I accepted Mark's offer and joined him on the terrace with a bit of anxiety as to what I was about to get myself into. Mark took the joint and held it up to his mouth and began to inhale the smoke from the rolled up paper. I watched very closely to see exactly what he was going to do. After he held the smoke in his mouth for a few seconds he exhaled and a plume of smoke came out of his mouth and he smiled and offered the joint to me.

Trying to mimic his actions, I held the joint between the appropriate fingers and took a huge puff off of the marijuana filled cigarette. After one hit I started to cough uncontrollably and he told me there was an easier way to do it and he then proceeded to give me a shotgun hit. Not knowing what that was, I braced myself for a sudden hit to the back of the head.

Mark then took the joint and drew in a big mouth full of the smoke and held it within him. Right after that, he moved towards me with his mouth just inches away from mine. He took his hand, held my cheeks and moved in towards me as if he was going to kiss me. As I stood there waiting to see what happened next, he began to blow the smoke into my mouth and instructed me to swallow and hold it in for a few seconds. When I exhaled I had the most comfortable feeling I had ever experienced and that was when he kissed me.

Moments later we found ourselves running to his apartment where he placed my drunken body on his bed and began to undress me. Drunk, and now stoned, I simply laid there on his bed as he unrobed and placed his body on top of mine. At first I said no to him but when I felt his hands unbuckling my belt and felt his tongue caressing my abdominal area, I knew there would be no turning back. When he began to kiss me I started feeling as if the room was spinning. He assured me that everything would be alright and I submitted to him. The next few hours were filled with passion and desire that I could only imagine prior to that night.

When I awoke the next morning Mark was still sleeping so I gathered my belongings and ran as quickly as I could across the campus to Kirsten's room where I was hoping to find her. As I rushed across the lush green grass on the bright sunny morning, I was terrified. What had I done? Not only had I had sex with another man, but I had smoked pot and possibly lost one of the best friends I ever had.

When I found Kirsten, she expressed concern and said that she had been worried all night that I had been kidnapped. Not having the courage to tell her what had actually happened, I simply said that I had gone to see a guys art work and that we ended up passing out in his floor. The look on her face told me that she didn't really believe my story, but neither did she want to know the truth.

Shortly after telling my untruth to Kirsten, I got in my car and made the long journey home where I jumped in the shower and tried to wash my guilt away.

It would be several years before I would see Kirsten again. The guilt and shame of what I had done began to eat a hole in our friendship and gradually there was a distance between us that couldn't be sewn back together without a lot of time to heal.

As I was preparing for the rest of my life, the next stage would be college. Ashley and I had started seeing each other casually again and I was at her house one evening and began to talk to her mother about college and how I would like to find one that would help me to straighten out my life and get back on the path of righteousness. She had the answer: It was a Church of God college in a small town in Tennessee. ⁓

Change is defined as: "To make different in some particular, to make radically different, or to give a different position, course, or direction".

As the world changes around us, we have no choice but to change with it. Change is inevitable and with it comes possibility. It is in the light of change that we find ourselves evolving and traveling in different directions. With just a little faith and perseverance we can learn to depend on change to lead us in the direction of fulfillment and find a place to belong.

Don't be afraid of change but, rather, embrace it. The bad will find you; it is up to you to seek the good. With each change in life EXPECT…

Chapter Three
"Self Realization"

⟿⟿

**"The ethical theory that the highest good for man
consists in realizing or fulfilling himself usually
on the assumption that he has certain inborn
abilities constituting his real or ideal self."**

S elf realization occurs most often when fear and doubt
are relinquished. It sometimes happens without much
effort and usually follows a major change in your life. With self
realization comes the feeling of freedom and deliverance. As is
implied in the actual term, the actual self alone must find this
euphoria and sense of well being.

It isn't often easy to realize one's self and self realization
does not come without some amount of concerted effort. To
realize one's self is freedom. Freedom from the fear of rejection,
from the fear of failure and, most importantly, freedom to love.
To love not only someone else, but to love yourself. When you

learn to accept yourself and then love yourself, you can safely begin the wonderful journey of finding someone else to love.

~ Upon arrival at the school that I had decided would change my life and help me to become the person that I thought I should be, I knew immediately that I had made the right decision. The people were all so friendly and willing to help me find my way around campus. Everyone carried a Bible and spoke of God's love and divine plan for me.

The rules were spelled out in detail in the handbook, as well as the repercussions for breaking the rules. They were very strict and there was no room for discussion of the rules as they were deemed as 'God's rules'. There was no way I could fail on this mission of turning my life around.

Within two days I had already found a girlfriend. She was tall, dark haired and absolutely beautiful. Elise was everything a guy could want in a girl.

We met for the first time in the commons. She walked by and smiled at me and I sent her my most flirtatious smile in return and before the smile could vanish she spoke to me and said, "Do you know how hot you are?" With that, I knew I had my girlfriend and now had only the task of finding out what God's plan was for me.

It wasn't long after our first meeting that Elise asked me if I liked to party. Without hesitation, I simply said yes and we were off to find a bottle of wine (which led to my first visit to the Dean's office).

Elise and I were together every waking moment for the first few weeks of school and I knew that she was falling in love with me and I wanted so badly for the same feelings towards her, but those feelings just weren't developing within me. Wanting a sense of what everyone around me saw as normality was my only wish but I still fell asleep at night with thoughts of another man next to me.

Old Testament was a mandatory class for all freshmen and it bored me to tears…until I saw an incredibly handsome guy looking at me. He was sitting on the opposite side of the room from me and we couldn't keep our eyes off of each other from that moment on. His hair was jet black, his eyes sparkled with every glance and his smile made everything else in the room disappear.

Parker and I glanced at each other every couple of seconds during class and following that was the smile that says, "I'd really like to get to know you". After a few days of glancing, looking away and glancing back, he approached me after class and said, "I think I missed a few things in class today. Could I borrow your notes?" Without hesitation I offered him my notebook and he was on his way and all I could think of after that was his smell. I wanted to take it with me everywhere I went. Calvin Klein's 'Obsession' was what Parker wore, and I was already obsessed.

That day in class, the professor had mentioned in his lecture that the name 'Ben' means 'son of'. In my notes I tried to entertain myself during that grueling lecture and above the new bit of trivia I had learned I wrote the words "Ben a Bitch".

The next day before class, Parker came in and handed me my notebook and gave me the smile that I had adored the day before and then he made my day…he sat down right next to me. I didn't hear a word from the professor that day because I could only focus on this beautiful and mesmerizing person that was right next to me. Every time I inhaled, his cologne rushed through me like an intoxicating drug.

After class Parker looked at me and said, "Don't forget to look over your notes from yesterday" as he shook my hand and expressed how thankful he was that I let him borrow my notes. Then he walked away and all I could do was just stand there and watch. Then he turned back and gave me that inebriating smile once more.

When I got back to my room, I found myself smelling my notebook to see if it smelled like him. When I opened it, he had written these words over my banter about Ben: "That is too funny! We should get together for a most excellent party sometime" and below that was his phone number.

After I had exhausted myself from jumping up and down with excitement, I mustered up the nerve to call the number Parker had written in my notebook and was relieved to get his voicemail. The message I left was simple: "Parker, it's Ben. Call me back if you'd like. I'm very interested in that party."

The two hours that followed that seemed like days. With the fear of missing Parker's call, I couldn't leave my room. Finally the phone rang and it was him. He offered to pick me up and asked if I would like to join him for dinner, and eagerly I accepted the offer.

As I was frantically searching for the perfect clothes for my date with Parker, there was a knock at my window. As I pulled the blinds up, I realized it was Elise. "Shit! What am I going to do about that?" I had been so preoccupied with thoughts of Parker, she hadn't even entered my mind and I had plans to go out with her that night as well. Without missing a beat, I told her that there was a campus choir meeting that I had forgotten about and I was running late and I would call her later.

When there was finally a knock on my door, I raced towards it and opened it and saw Parker standing there waiting to take me away. I could hardly speak at that very moment. He was a dream come true and he was standing right in front of me.

He drove me to a restaurant in Chattanooga and was the gentleman that I had always envisioned in my dreams. He ordered wine and suggested items from the menu that would enhance it's essence. He listened to every word I said and remarked on every comment. The dinner was perfect and I didn't want that night to ever end.

When we were back in the car and on the way back to campus, Parker looked at me and said, "Would you like to see something spectacular?" Of course my answer was yes, so he turned around and drove me to Lookout Mountain where we sat and drank a bottle of white grenache, looked at the stars and the city below us, and talked about our lives and where we wanted them to go.

When the last of the wine was gone, Parker looked at me and said, "I would very much like to kiss you right now". I replied, "I think you'd better". The kiss lasted for a very long time and it was the first kiss I had ever had that made my insides turn warm. This man was going to take my heart and I was willingly going to give it to him.

The drive home went by very quickly as I knew this night was rapidly coming to an end. Parker's hand held mine the entire way and I was happier than I had ever been before. When we arrived back to the campus he kissed me once more and drove away.

As I stood there watching his car disappear into the distance I realized that there was no hiding from this anymore.

If I wasn't gay, I couldn't be feeling this way, and just as I was turning to enter the dorms, Elise walked up to me and said, "Where have you been?"

As Parker and I became closer, a distance grew between Elise and me. She was hurt and angry, and rightfully so. She had no idea what was going on and I didn't have the courage to tell her. After many lies, she eventually gave up on me and found other friends and someone else to love.

Parker and I continued to see each other as much as possible and fall more deeply in love each day. Each time I saw him it was just like the first. Each time I looked into his eyes I fell for him all over again. Every time Parker made love to me I felt that the sun had just risen for the first time and I wanted to share the magic of that feeling with the rest of the world. These feelings were so natural and real that they made me know within my heart that there was nothing wrong with me. There was simply no way that these feelings could live within me, alongside my love for God, and still be a sin.

Parker and I both struggled deeply within our souls to understand what was going on. We had been told all of our lives that what we were feeling and experiencing was evil and an abomination in the sight of God.

It was required by the college that students must attend chapel three times per week. With this being a Church of God college, chapel wasn't like any ordinary chapel service. There was praying in tongues, jumping up and down, shouting, raising hands, the laying on of hands to deliver believers from their burdens and non-believers from their sins; and there was singing. Lots and lots of singing. The songs and styles of the Church of God are designed in such a way that they summon such emotion from inside a soul that they could make Darwin himself jump out of his grave and shout hallelujah to the good Lord Almighty.

One specific night in chapel was to begin the downfall of the physical manifestations of Parker's love for me. It was, for me, chapel as usual. But something changed inside of Parker that night.

We met at our usual spot and walked to Parker's car and I thought we were going to drive to the secret place that we so often went to and talked about our love for each other and kissed each other until the wee hours of the morning. This night was to be another pinnacle in my search for my inner happiness.

When Parker took my hand that night in the darkness of his car, I felt that something had changed. His eyes welled up with tears as he began to speak to me and tell me that he loved me with all of his heart, but he felt that we had been doing something that was terribly wrong. He told me that I should go to Elise and ask for her forgiveness and that he was going to ask a girl out from choir that he had known since his childhood.

Feeling like I simply wanted to suffocate, I asked him to take me home and reconsider his thoughts and find out where his true feelings were coming from. He then drove me back to my dorm and kissed me goodnight one final time.

Months went by with me having to see him in class, pass him on the campus, and see him with that poor girl that I was sure would be heartbroken in the not so distant future. It was during those months that I began to make even more bad decisions.

There was a group of students that I had seen around campus that were rumored to sneak out at night and drive to Chattanooga and visit the gay bars there. They were to become my new circle of friends and going to the bars was my new form of entertainment.

Parker continued to call and wanted to talk about how to change my life and to tell me how he missed me and wished that things could be different. By that point I had accepted who I was, and with the help of my new friends, I couldn't listen to another dramatic story about how God was working in Parker's life and how he knew that I would find happiness and fulfillment someday. For the time being I was happy. Or so I thought.

Going to the bars every night and finding numerous men to 'fall in love with', began to take over my life and that eventually led to me failing out of school.

Indeed, I had accepted the fact that I was gay but I had forgotten about the other aspects of my life. Most of my thoughts were consumed earlier by realizing who I was and defending that to the point of heart break. Fear of being gay was no longer going to define me and that was all that I had focused on, which led to the fact that I still needed to find out who else I was, and what I was supposed to do with the rest of my life.~

Self realization is a multi-layered occurrence. It does not only begin to define who you are as a person, but it should also help you discover that being gay does not define you: what does define you is what you contribute to society and the people that you come in contact with and what you leave behind.

The most important ingredient of self realization is the power that it gives you to begin the journey of life that is yours to direct and navigate to the destination of your ideal self. This sense of well-being is your gift to yourself; the power that is given to you because of it is your gift to those around you and, ultimately, the world.

The natural inborn abilities that you were given have been realized and now it is up to you to put them into action to be the change that you want to see in your own world. Once you begin to put all of this into practice you will begin to be on your way to EXPECT…

Chapter Four
"Courage"

———✦✦✦———

(Mental or moral strength to venture, persevere, and withstand danger, fear or difficulty)

With self-realization comes an overwhelming sense of accomplishment and readiness to take on the world. After you fight the battle of accepting who you are it becomes obvious to you that you now have the power to change the people that surround you which, in turn, changes your environment and state of well-being. Self-realization will give you a strong emotional self reliance.

Courage enables you to fight your battles on your own and not cower down to the remarks that others make out of ignorance. It permits you to be strong and stand on your own against your foes. Courage strengthens the spirit and allows it to persevere through rejection and rise above self-doubt and hatred.

All of the world will not accept you as you are, but with courage you will find the tenacity to move forward with your own life and before you know it you will ultimately find that people begin to see the new you and actually respect you for being who you are: just as you are.

~ On the last day I was to walk the campus grounds of the Church of God College, I was awakened by a knock on my door. When I opened it I was dismayed to see who had initiated the opening of my eyes that morning. There before me stood my parents! The college was four hours away from home and I knew something drastic had to be the reason for this surprise visit.

My parents had found themselves doubting my answer to "How is school going?". When queried by my parents over many phone calls, my response to the question would simply be a quick reply of, "Fine." and I would suddenly move on to another topic.

To my dismay, my parents had called the Dean of Academics and found out the real answer to their worrisome questions. When told that my grades were not sufficient and I had been asked to report to the Dean's office on several occasions, they quickly sprang into action and drove to Tennessee and removed me from the school.

The next few months would seem quite trying as I realized that I may never see Parker or any of my new friends again and now must move on with my life and figure out what to do with myself and find new people that would understand and appreciate me.

Parker and I would talk on the phone at least once per day and that is what resulted in the shot heard 'round the world as soon as my mother opened the first phone bill.

Nearly a month had gone by since I had returned back to my hometown and Parker had again pledged his love to me and we would talk for hours about how we were going to work it out so that we could be together again. When my mother rushed through my bedroom door on that morning I will never forget, she looked like a mad woman as she was waving a piece of paper in the air and screaming, "How could you run up a five-hundred goddamned dollar phone bill?!

That was the first time I had ever heard my Mother use profanity; especially to that level. All I could manage to think was, "I'm screwed! Baptists don't use that word…ever!" Soon thereafter it was time for me to find a job.

Realizing that my new found courage was still quite vulnerable and could possibly succumb to the judgments of small town thinking, I drove to the nearest large city in search of employment and accepted a job as a Sales Associate at one of the larger department stores in the mall there.

It wasn't long before I found a group of people with similar interests as mine and we became quite a tight crowd. It didn't take them long to introduce me to the gay bars in Winston-Salem and I was off and running towards the man of my dreams…once again.

After many one night stands with various guys I would meet in the bars, I was bewildered and amused by a phone call I received at work one day. On the other end of the line was a deep and sexy voice asking me if I was interested in meeting him for dinner some night. With little hesitation and much intrigue, I said that I was indeed interested in a rendezvous and the plans were made. The instructions were for me to go to one of the restaurants in the mall after work, have a seat at the bar, and ask for Jackson.

The last few hours at work that day were filled with anticipation as I awaited the time for me to be relieved of my duties so that I could go and meet with my mystery man.

As I took my seat at the bar, I saw a somewhat familiar face across the bar looking back at me. Quickly, my mind began to wonder if that was Jackson. I had seen him several times in the store where I worked. There was always a certain look that he would give me that was very recognizable. It was the same look I used to receive from Parker in Old Testament class. There was also something else I had noticed about him: his wife and son.

As soon as I had remembered all of this, he got up from his seat and started towards me. Jackson was a beautiful man with shimmering black hair that just brushed his shoulders, the most intense dark brown eyes, and skin that was the color of an island surfer and that skin covered the most perfectly formed muscles I had seen on a real person. His tight, red Polo shirt did nothing but enhance the appearance of his bulging arms and chest.

Immediately, I began to wonder if Jackson just happened to be in the bar having a drink while he waited for his wife. A feeling of embarrassment rushed through me as I thought, "What if he comes over and sits next to me to chat while I wait for my mysterious stranger to approach me?" and soon after that he was standing next to me with his hand outstretched and introduced himself as Jackson.

After several draft beers and much small talk about work and weather, I summoned up the nerve to ask him about his wife and his son. The look in his eyes was that of bewilderment and he asked me how I knew about them. Not realizing that I had been admiring him while he shopped, Jackson was flattered to hear that I had noticed him as well. He then told me that he had recently moved into an apartment and was soon to be divorced. With that news I felt the need to inform him that I had no interest in dating a married man. Having no experience on that field, I could only go by what my friends had told me, "Never date a married man. It's much worse in the gay world than it is the straight world. You will never get your man!".

Over the course of the next few weeks, Jackson would come by the store and ask me to go to dinner with him and finally I agreed. After all, he was hot!

The date we agreed upon arrived and I met Jackson at his apartment where we sat and had a glass of wine and talked for a short while before leaving for dinner. He seemed like a perfect guy thus far, but the thoughts of his wife and kid were still in the back of my mind.

We had dinner at a fairly nice restaurant downtown and we also had more than one bottle of wine. The more wine that I had, the less important his marital status became, and with that, the more inviting his lips and arms were to me.

It was late by the time we got back to his apartment and I knew that I had too much to drink to drive an hour back home and he asked me to come in for a night-cap. I had recently discovered that the term night-cap is defined as an alcoholic beverage consumed at bedtime and began to giggle. When Jackson asked what was so amusing to me, I told him of the trivia that was in my present thought and just before he kissed me he said, "That's exactly how I would define it".

The kiss lasted all the way to Jackson's bedroom and with each step toward that room, an article of clothing was removed and left in our smoldering trail. By the time we landed on the bed, we were completely unclothed and filled with such a thirst for each other that we skipped the small talk and went straight for it. The way he moved was unlike anything I had ever known. He held my arms above my head and took me to a sexual place that was intended for lovers that had know each other for decades.

The next morning came very quickly and I awoke with many varied and apprehensive emotions. The night had been extraordinary. Jackson was an incredible lover, there was no questioning that. The troubling thoughts were guilt and fear. The guilt was because he was still married; the fear was from thinking about my parents. I was old enough to be out on my own but I still lived with my parents and they were more than concerned and loving parents They were worriers of the worst sort. They were the kind of worriers that worry led to fear and fear led to anger, and anger was what was bestowed upon me for worrying them.

Back in high school I had learned a very useful trick that worked every time I was going to be out later than I should: Wherever I was, I would simply find a quiet place to use a phone and would dial my parents number. When my mother would answer the phone I would simply say, "It's okay, Mom. I've got it." Content that I was safe at home and in my room, she would roll over and go back to sleep. How had I forgotten to do that this time? Knowing I was headed for a verbal beating, I grabbed my belongings and slipped out the door and headed home.

After the long drive home and the anticipated verbal bashing, I had to get ready, turn around and go back to work.

When I arrived to work I noticed a vase of red roses on one of the cashier stands and thought about how nice it would be to receive flowers at work that were sent just because someone was thinking about me and, much to my surprise, the card had my name on it. These words were written inside the card: "Please forgive me if I upset you. Why did you leave without saying goodbye? Please give me a chance and meet me at the bar after work."

Needless to say, I ran from work to the other end of the mall towards the bar where I found Jackson waiting for me. He told me that he was enamored with me and would do whatever it took to make me his.

The next few weeks we were together every night. It was the best few weeks I had enjoyed since I had been with Parker. We were in love and decided that it was time to take things a step further and move in together. There was an over-garage apartment behind my sister's house that was available and that is where we decided to move and make our first home together, and that is when things began to change.

Being in that small North Carolina town was difficult enough when you were alone and people only suspected that you were gay, but to actually have a partner seemed to be a slap in the face for most of the town folk.

The judgmental stares and remarks made it difficult for Jackson and I to have the life that we had so hoped for. We were in love and wanted everyone to share in our joy but it just wasn't the time in that little town.

Through perseverance and courage, we managed to go about our daily lives, in the midst of the surrounding hatred and ignorance, and live in harmony with each other for the better part of a year.

Jackson had begun to show a lot of jealousy towards my family, friends, and even my work. It became clear that I was to do nothing but come straight home to him every day. With no real self knowledge of the actions of love, I thought that it was normal and was actually flattered that Jackson wanted me all to himself.

My father had wondered why I spent all of my time with Jackson and eventually asked if we were gay. The question, once out there, seemed to dangle like a two-edged sword before it actually reached from my father's lips to my ears. I wanted so badly to be able to say, "Yes, Daddy…and we are in love!" but my courage just didn't seem to be at that level yet and I could only lie and tell him that he must be crazy to think such a thing.

After I got home that afternoon and told Jackson about the big question, we began discussing the fact that it was indeed time for us to tell my parents and, after that, the world. Over the next few days Jackson became very adamant that we needed to go and tell my parents about our situation and our love.

The day arrived that Jackson and I had decided to be the one when we were to unload our burden of secrecy to my parents and I was filled with anxiety the entire day. As I took the first step and picked up the phone to call my mother and tell her that Jackson and I had something we needed to talk to her and my father about, I felt a hand grasp my shoulder and Jackson's voice telling me to be strong. The words came out easily enough. When I told my Mother we needed to talk, she was very calm and simply said, "That's no problem. We'll be home tonight. Come on over."

As Jackson and I entered my parents home, I felt like I was going to throw up. My parents were sitting in their usual chairs where they would often watch Jeopardy after dinner so Jackson and I joined them and sat down on the sofa next to each other and I began to speak.

"Daddy, do you remember what you asked me the other day?" I said, as my voice trembled. Daddy's response was a simple but acute "What about, son?" and I replied, "About Jackson and I being gay." and I knew right then that we were headed for fireworks.

The sharp and pointed words that were fired through the air at that moment were like a personal Pearl Harbor. As both of my parents sat straight up in their chairs at the same time and began shouting at us, I knew that this decision was going to result in a very strenuous relationship for everyone involved. Simultaneously, my parents were shouting. My father's first remarks were, "Good God! Screwing each other in the ass! It didn't come from this side of the family!" as my mother was screaming every scripture that she had in her arsenal of biblical knowledge concerning the subject. And I wept.

The shouting continued for several minutes before I decided that it was time to leave. Taking Jackson by the hand, I led him to the door and turned with tears in my eyes to say goodbye to my parents, not knowing if I would ever be welcome in their home again.

When we reached our apartment, my sister was waiting in the driveway and announced that she just received a phone call from our mother and she asked if she could speak to me for a moment. With a quick glance at Jackson, I mumbled, "Jesus! I can't go through this twice in one night." and he urged me to give her audience.

As soon as I reached my sister, she stretched out her arms and told me she knew that I had just come from a difficult situation and then she hugged me. She then proceeded to tell me that when mom had hysterically tried to describe the scene that was still only moments behind me, my sister asked only one question: "Is he happy?". That thought hadn't entered my mother's mind as all the information she had about homosexuality was that it was a disease and her son had it and was surely destined for eternal damnation.

With new tears in my eyes, my sister looked at me and simply asked, "Well, are you happy?". After I assured her that I was indeed happier than I had been in some time, she pushed me away and said, "That's all that matters to me. Go get Jackson and we'll make cookies."

The next few hours gave me a comfort that I had never known. Being there in my sisters kitchen with her and my boyfriend was the first glimpse of the world that I had always wanted to live in. I had at least one family member that now knew everything there was to know about me and she loved me…she really loved me. No fire on a cold winter night could touch the warmth that my sister's love afforded me that night as we stood in her kitchen, baking cookies, drinking wine and actually laughing together and twenty years later, every time I smell cookies baking in the oven, I am taken back to that moment when I felt what it was like to be loved unconditionally.

The next few weeks were very hard as I had no idea what to do as I was so accustomed to calling my mom or my dad just to say hi, or to drive to their house and sit with them and have a cup of coffee. Those times were gone and I didn't know if I would ever have them back.

Days went by with no communication with my parents and I had never felt an emptiness in my life as I did during those days. Nearly a week later, I discovered that my parents also felt an emptiness within them. One phone call set the healing on course as my mother called and we talked for hours about what I had revealed to them. She and my father had talked a lot about it and neither of them understood it, but they were willing to try. All that mattered to them was that I was their son, and no matter what, they loved me.

As the seemingly endless process of mending a broken relationship between a son and his parents began, it became more and more apparent that this was not what Jackson wanted. When the subject of my parents came up, or the mentioning of my going to meet them for lunch or dinner occurred, He became quite defensive and assured me that they were only out for reconciliation with me for the simple task of driving a wedge between him and myself and that it was their mission to come between us and separate us.

The courage of love enabled my parents and me to begin having somewhat normal conversations again and even to laugh together. Jackson never attended any of our meetings and anger became his weapon.

It was pointed out to me that Jackson had shut me off from all of my friends and it was his intent to separate me from my family as well. Being flustered by the fact that my sister did not react in a negative way but, rather supported us, his madness began to manifest itself physically.

The first time I picked myself up off of the bathroom floor after being forced there by the power of Jackson's hand, I realized that it was time to put my courage to work and learn to direct my own life and move forward into the unknown world and find my place to belong.

When the police officer arrived at our apartment, I walked out of my sister's house, climbed the stairs to the apartment, and was met by a shouting mad man. "How can you do this to me? I love you! I can't believe you're leaving me!" When his hand raised against me, the officer walked in behind me and assured Jackson that it would not be in his best interest to interfere with me as I gathered my belongings.

Without saying a word to him, I walked out of his life and into my own.~

Courage doesn't come easily but it is essential to developing a sense of self worth and it is vital to becoming the person that you strive to be. It allows you to stand before others and declare that you are an individual who is worthy of their love and respect.

With courage, you can grow to become confident in your own belief system and overcome the judgments of others who simply can't see you for who you are. Courage is like a muscle, it must be exercised in order to grow.

With a few simple acts of faith and believing in your own courage, you can undoubtedly EXPECT…

Chapter Five
"Strength"

——ཉ∿ཉ——

(Degree of potency of effect or of concentration)

While courage is a stepping stone to the mental state of being strong, strength is the building block for enabling you to make difficult and life changing decisions. Inevitably, at some point in every person's life, there comes a time when a difficult decision must be made in order to obtain the happiness that one deserves in life. Protein is to a muscle as courage is to strength. It is an essential ingredient in a life that desires and chooses to find a life of fulfillment and joy.

Inner strength allows you to make decisions and carry them out that may not be what others see as being the best for you. It allows you to say, "This is what I feel is best for me. It may hurt or confuse you at the time, but eventually, you will see it is for the best".

You can overcome fear, withstand change, realize who you are deep within and gain courage, but having inner strength and believing in yourself, when others may not, gives you the tenacity and willpower to move forward and discover just how great life can really be. Especially for someone as unique as you are. You walk with courage, but run with strength.

~ The decision to leave Jackson was necessarily a quick one which left me no time for a plan other than to move back in with my parents until I got back on my feet and discovered what I was going to do next. Life has a way of sending you to the right places at the right time if you allow it to.

Over the next few months, my parents and I were able to heal the wounds that had been inflicted upon our relationship and eventually we learned to love each other more than we had before. The realization that I was something other than what my parents thought I was had been a difficult discovery, but one worth exploring for them. We had several months to reconnect while I was staying with them but that began to be a challenging situation.

The need to be around people who really understood me led me back to my friends and the bars and almost every night after work, I would head out to dinner with them and then out to the bars. It would often times be rather late in the night before I would return home and my parents began worrying and even sitting up and waiting for me to return. After a while, I made the decision that it was time for me to look for a place of my own and I began searching.

After I found a small apartment that I could afford, an hour and a half away from home in Greensboro, North Carolina, it was time to tell the news to my parents. They weren't happy about me moving out of town, but they realized that it was time for me to move on. The love of my parents could be seen by some (especially a professional therapist) as a bit abnormal. I found it to be extremely comforting. I was very fortunate to have a strong bond with my family and I knew what it was like to almost lose it. Having a few friends who no longer had contact with their families simply because they were gay gave me a great sense of being grateful for what I had with my mom, dad and sister.

My new life had begun and it was beginning to be one hell of a ride. There was hardly a night that went by that I wasn't on a date with a different guy. There were so many to choose from and I was like a kid in a candy store. The bars in Winston-Salem seemed to offer up not only gay men, but good looking gay men. Toto, I wasn't in Kansas anymore!

With the fear of becoming too involved with any single man because of what I had been through with Jackson, I would tend to go out with someone once or twice and then tell them that I was no longer interested. The constant thoughts of becoming the person that I was with Jackson kept me from becoming the person that I wanted to be. More than anything, I wanted someone there by my side; someone that I could share the intimate details of my life with.

It was quite a few months before I grew tired of waking up with a stranger lying next to me and I began to wonder if this was what the rest of my life would be. Often times I would talk to my friends about my feelings and they would simply laugh and tell me to be thankful as it had been weeks since they had been laid.

While I was weaving my tapestry of sordid men, I still felt lonely inside and, just in time, I met Sean. His presence alone demanded the attention of a crowded room. He stood a couple of inches above everyone else in the room and his black hair and dazzling blue eyes seemed to penetrate every person he looked at…and he was looking at me. As he approached me in the smoke filled bar, I could only imagine that he was going to pass by and speak to someone else but, the closer he got, the more I realized his gaze was focused on my longing eyes.

Sean and I talked for hours. He was the most interesting person I had ever engaged in conversation. He was a student at the local university and offered insight and views to subjects of life that I had never thought of. He talked about politics and how active he was in that scene and, being completely ignorant of any of it, I could only sit and listen intently to his every word. When I was growing up, you were either Democrat or Republican, that was it, and you didn't question either one as to why.

Sean had recently come out to his closest friends and was struggling to find a balance between his romantic life and the life he still desired to maintain with his straight entourage. His friends weren't expecting him to bring someone like me around. They were expecting someone more like Sean: athletic, intellectual and, a term I learned later: Straight Acting.

The welcome surprise of acceptance came from his ex-girlfriend. Sarah seemed to be quite intrigued by the whole situation and would ask me to join her for lunch and shopping excursions. I soon became her token gay and we had many laughs together comparing our experiences with Sean, which seemed to puzzle him.

It had been Sean's dream for several years to move to Atlanta because the Olympics were going to be there and his greatest desire at that point in his life was to be a part of it. After long and detailed discussions about our relationship and where we were headed with it, we both decided that Atlanta would be the perfect place for us to start all over together and that was what we were going to do.

The decision to move to Atlanta did not come without the shedding of more tears. As I told my parents that I would be leaving for Atlanta, it was as if I had told them I was moving to the moon. Atlanta seemed so far away from home but I assured them that they would see me very often. The big city was, after all, only a four and a half hour drive.

The day finally came that Sean and I were to set off on our big adventure and I watched in the rear view mirror as my mom, dad and sister became smaller and smaller in the reflective glass. We were off to discover our brand new lives in a brand new and exciting place.

As we drove into Atlanta in the rented U-Haul on Highway eighty-five, Sean and I both began to cheer. The skyline seemed to welcome us and announce the glorious life the city had in store for us.

When we first walked into the leasing office to sign for our new apartment, I was a bit nervous about the leasing agent realizing that Sean and I were a couple and I knew that it was obvious as we had leased a one bedroom apartment. But my fear soon diminished as the extremely kind and welcoming lady began to discuss the details of the lease and then proceeded to tell us what a great city Atlanta was for gay people and even offered us directions to some of the gay bars. I couldn't believe it! Back at home everything had to be behind closed doors but now we were in a great big city that actually celebrated us. This new world was sure to be just what I had searched for my entire life.

We began moving in what few earthly belongings we had accumulated up until that point of our young lives, and before long we were famished so we decided to take a break and find the nearest super market and buy some food and bring it back and cook our first dinner together in our first apartment as a happy couple.

Grocery stores had never interested me as I only saw them as a source of nourishment and future labor but this one was different. The foods to select from were mind boggling to me. There were foods from all over the world to choose from and I found it difficult to find the very few basic things that I thought I knew how to cook at the time. There were at least a dozen different choices for potatoes and I only really knew of one kind: the big white ones that are intended for baking or mashing. After a few minutes of staring at potatoes, we made our selection and headed for the poultry department which seemed to be a mile away but in the same store. Along the way to find the chicken breasts we both stopped in awe as we turned down the beer and wine aisle. This aisle that was dedicated to the nectar of the gods was as large as the entire super markets back home that I was accustomed to. We shortly thereafter picked our jaws up out of the floor and realized that we were faced with a very important decision. "Which wine should we select for our very first dinner in our new home?" Finally we spotted a familiar bottle, Robert Mondavi was to be our liquid guest that evening.

Perhaps the most amazing thing to me about this store was the fact that there were other people that seemed to be just like Sean and me. There were same-sex couples shopping together mixed in amongst the heterosexual housewives and occasional bewildered husband that had been sent there to buy some certain last minute item. And they all seemed to get along just fine, side by side shopping for sustenance.

Two hours later, we were back in the apartment and I began to get things ready for dinner while Sean put the bed together and unpacked a few more boxes.

With little to no knowledge of how to cook, I stood staring at the pots and pans and wondered which were appropriate for potatoes, chicken breasts and broccoli. Soon thereafter I found myself pleased with my decisions and began boiling water in the large pot that was now intended to yield mashed potatoes in a short while.

Three hours had gone by since I began boiling the potatoes and Sean began inquiring as to what was taking so long. "We must have gotten a funny sort of potato because they just won't soften and they've been boiling for over an hour" was my defense. Sean's next move was to remove the lid from the pot and check the stubborn potatoes for himself. "Jesus Christ! No wonder!" he exclaimed as he proceeded to tell me that I should have sliced the potatoes before submerging them into the water.

Our first dinner in our first home together consisted of two bottles of cabernet sauvignon, a six-pack of beer and pizza that was conveniently delivered right to our door. For the rest of the night, we laid in the floor, holding each other closely, talking about our dreams in the big city, and smiling.

Over the next few days Sean and I began searching for jobs and soon we were both working in different restaurants as servers. It didn't take us long to find out that the service industry is where most gay men begin their working lives. There was even a joke about Atlanta that went something like this: How many straight waiters in Atlanta does it take to screw in a light bulb? The answer was: both of them.

Sean and I both began to make friends at work and we were both very happy with each other and with our growing family of friends for many months before things began to change.

The restaurant that Sean was working in was much more upscale than the chain restaurant that I had chosen to be my place of employment and the people employed by each establishment were quite different as well. Not only did the patrons from Sean's restaurant see themselves as superior to those of mine, but the staff seemed to share that same vision of grandeur and it became clear that neither the twain shall meet.

It was during a small cocktail party that Sean and I had put together that the simple clash of the classes became pointedly clear. Not long into the soiree, I noticed that there was one side of the room filled with Sean's work mates, and another side filled with mine. And we were separated as well.

The air that night was filled with judgment from each side of the room and I grew more and more uncomfortable with it with each passing moment.

After our guests had left I asked Sean if he felt the discomfort in the room that I had experienced. He said that he had no idea what I was talking about and I began to explain it to him. His reply was quite unsettling to me as he informed me that his friends were a bit more civilized than mine were. After the disappointment of his answer settled in I began to wonder how this could be. We were, after all, coming from similar backgrounds of having to deal with prejudices and bullying. Why should such things exist in our own community? It seemed clear to me that we should all be standing by one another in support of each other and helping the other out in times of need. That was not the general consensus among the different subcultures that I was beginning to learn about.

The next day at work was filled with questions from my fellow workers. "What are you doing hanging out with those pompous assholes?" was the most frequently asked and it made me start to wonder: Are Sean and I truly compatible? Did he see himself as being better than me? I couldn't stand the questions that were ringing inside of my head and I needed to have the answers to them.

The answers came one by one and were quite obvious. As Sean began spending more time with his friends and I began to spend more with mine, we began to grow further and further apart.

The beginning of the end of our relationship began on a cold and rainy night. With a fever running over 100 degrees I decided to stay at home and was in hopes that Sean would stay with me to comfort me while I wasn't feeling well. That wasn't to be as he had made plans to go to a local bar and watch a basketball game with some of his friends, and as he walked out the door, he said that he would be home right after the game.

At home on the couch I turned the television on to watch the game that Sean had gone to see with his friends and decided to open up a bottle of wine and began to drink it. Before long, I realized I had consumed the entire bottle of wine. That, mixed with the Nyquil that I had taken turned out to be a nearly fatal mistake.

The game had been over for two hours before Sean returned home and I asked him where the hell he had been. His reply of "I didn't feel like coming home right after the game so we had a few more beers" didn't sit well in my mind with the influence of the bottle of wine and the Nyquil. An angry side of me that I had never seen before began to surface and before I knew it, I had reached for a heavy glass ashtray that was on the coffee table and threw it directly at him. Fortunately, he ducked as it whizzed by his head and lodged itself into the sheetrock on the wall. After the initial shock wore off Sean asked me if I had lost my mind and I began to laugh hysterically. That didn't sit well with Sean and he began to swear uncontrollably at me.

That night as we laid in bed, not speaking, there was a line from a book that Kathie Lee Gifford had written that kept resounding in my head: "There is no greater distance than the distance between two people who are in the same bed and not in love". Those words would not leave my mind as I began to wonder if that was what Sean and I were, two people in the same bed who were not in love.

That night changed the dynamics of our relationship drastically and permanently. After that, our friends began to take us in opposite directions. Sean spent most of his time with his friends and I spent most of my time with mine.

Sean and I had become the equivalent of roommates and I soon found myself taking comfort in the arms of another man.

One of my friends had an apartment downtown and the complex was known to have mostly gay men residing there. The pool was always crowded with so many guys that it was sometimes impossible to find a place to lie on a towel and my friends and I spent most of our afternoons there.

One hot and sunny afternoon we were all by the pool drinking beer and having a great time and I looked across the pool and looking back at me was the most beautiful boy Atlanta had ever seen. He had short, dirty-blonde, wavy hair, sculpted arms, a chiseled chest and a smile that revealed perfectly straight teeth that were as white as the driven snow. Before long, this V-shaped Adonis of a man, with his tan and toned body, was walking straight towards me and then introduced himself as Brad.

Brad and I sat and talked for a solid hour. He had a sense of humor that kept me laughing the entire time. He had no reservations; if he thought it, he said it. That personality trait was so intriguing to me as I had always been one who worried about what other people thought of me. The laughter he afforded me was exactly what I had been needing for a very long time. When he asked me to join him later that night at one of the popular bars in town, I quickly said, "I would love to".

When I returned to the apartment later that evening I found a note on the table that said, "Gone out with friends, will be late, Sean". On the bottom of that note I replied, "Also gone out with friends, don't wait up".

After I put together the trendiest outfit my closet had to offer, I set out to the bar, Burkhart's, with my heart pounding from just thinking about this beautiful creature that already was consuming my every thought. The thoughts of his strong arms holding me and his full and powerful lips against mine made me weak at the knees.

As soon as I entered the bar I sensed his presence. It was only a few seconds until I felt Brad's hand on my shoulder and turned to see his bright and welcoming smile. We went to the bar and ordered a couple of beers and began talking. We talked for a couple of hours and decided to take a walk around the bar and see what all was going on.

There was a dark corner outside in the back of the bar and we paused there to talk a bit more. Before I knew it, this Goliath of a man had his hands around my waist and was lifting me up onto a table where he began to kiss me. It was a kiss like I'd never had before. With the power of his lips against mine and his very talented tongue, I could tell that he would be a very passionate lover. His hands knew precisely where I needed to be touched and his arms held me just where he wanted me.

Just as the kiss ended, I looked up to see Sean and his entourage looking right at us and in an instant I was sober and pulled myself away from Brad. I went over to Sean and it was almost as if he was relieved. He then introduced me to Scott. I had suspected for some time that there was something going on between the two of them and now I knew it.

When I turned around, Brad was still standing there waiting for me to return and I told Sean that I would meet him back at the apartment and we would talk about what we would do next concerning our relationship. Then I said goodnight to Brad and drove home where I found Sean waiting for me.

The conversation that Sean and I had that night was one of the most positive ones that we had had for quite a long time. We began to explore the reasons for our growing apart and realized that it was due to our own negligence and for allowing outside influences to guide us away from each other. A few tears were shed and it was agreed that, above all, we had been very good friends and would try to remain that way.

Sean kept the apartment and I found one of my own. Brad spent almost every night with me and we continued to have wonderful times together. We would spend afternoons in Piedmont Park simply watching people go by, sitting under the magnolia trees while holding hands and laughing.

The passion we shared was intense. Brad was extremely experimental and forceful in bed. Every time we had sex it was like a brand new experience. He was completely uninhibited and I found myself wanting more and more. It soon became clear that sex was all we had. The first time he told me that he loved me I had to pause and think before I could say it back, which I never did. I told him that I loved being with him but I also realized that we weren't of the same accord when it came to relationships. Those words hurt him, but he was willing to wait it out until I changed my mind.

Our passionate tryst lasted for several months until one day at work when I saw what I presumed to be the perfect guy for me. He came in with some of his co-workers for lunch and I couldn't keep my eyes off of him. He had beautiful, shiny blonde hair, radiant blue eyes and a captivating smile that was secretly directed at me every time I looked at him.

Our playful glances went back and forth during their entire lunch and when he was walking out the door, he turned to smile at me once more and he was gone.

As I was clearing their table I wondered if I would ever see him again. Then I saw his keys. He had left them behind underneath his napkin.

My shift was ending and I was getting ready to go home for the day so I gave the beautiful man's keys to a friend of mine and said, "I think this guy will come in later for these. Will you give them to him along with my number?" And that is what she did.

It was close to seven o'clock that evening and I was beginning to wonder if I had mistaken the look that the man in the blue suit had given me. Then the phone rang. The voice on the other end was so sweet and gentle as he introduced himself as Justin. My heart immediately began to race as I searched for the right words to say to him. He was very delicate but direct with his words and said that he would like to see me sometime. I assured him that I was very interested in the same opportunity and I made sure that the conversation didn't end until plans were definite.

The next night was to be our first date and we were going to meet at a local restaurant for drinks and dinner and that led to the difficult task of telling Brad that I was going to see another guy. That didn't go very well. Brad began to cry and told me that he would never let me go. It was painful to see him hurt but I knew that I had to be honest with him. I told him that it was simply time for me to start looking for someone that I could spend the rest of my life with and I was sorry that it wasn't him. Brad said he needed to be with me that night and he promised that he would change my mind. I agreed to be with him that night and we spent the entire night in bed. I knew that I would miss the way that he took me so fervently with his strong body, but I knew that I needed to love someone and it just couldn't be him.

The next evening when Justin picked me up I was filled with nervous energy. What if this is Mr. Right? I had to make sure I was on top of my game. The look had to be just right and the words must be well thought before delivered. The look was right, I could see it in his eyes when he first saw me. The words were another issue as nothing I said the entire evening came out as I had intended for it to. That seemed to be okay with Justin as he found it to be refreshing. He was surrounded with the corporate types all day and felt that it would be a welcome change to have a care-free spirit around.

The night went by quickly. We seemed to have so much in common. We were both from small towns and had struggled with much of the same issues. We both came from very strong family ties and that was the most important thing for me. All of the guys I had dated up until this point had never seemed to have strong connections with their families and it was often a struggle for them to understand my relationship with my family. Justin however, got it.

When Justin dropped me off at my apartment he said that he would very much like to see me again and gave me a very gentle kiss goodnight and drove away.

Strength can be found in the most unusual places. It can be found in the decision to just be friends. It can be found in the decision to be on your own for the very first time, in a new environment. You can find strength in the very first time you are honest with yourself and, honest with someone that has become closely involved with you. Strength offers you the ability to say no to someone even though it isn't what they want to hear.

Strength not only gives you the ability to protect yourself from hurt, but also affords you the ability of creating less damage to an already stressed relationship. Inner strength is the leader in the race to your own self-confidence and with it you can accomplish your life changing decisions without regret. With inner strength you can most often EXPECT…

Chapter Six
"Friendship"

———

(The quality or state of being friendly)

Webster's dictionary defines friendly as 'of, relating to, or befitting a friend: as showing kindly interest and goodwill'. A true friendship is not formed over night and sometimes it requires a lot of effort to find and hold a true friend. Some friendships happen simply by chance, whether it becomes a friendship formed through work or school, sometimes a person from your past reappears into your life and sometimes a true friendship is formed after a long romantic journey.

Wherever you find friendship, it is important to treat that person with kindness and respect. It is very difficult to mend a broken trust , but when you do, the friendship can sometimes be stronger than it ever was before. Forgiveness is one of the key ingredients to any relationship and it is a very liberating experience to learn how to forgive and exercise that act of kindness. At some point, we all need to be forgiven and we all need to forgive.

———

~ By the time I had been out with Justin a few times, Brad was beginning to get the fact that I had found a connection with someone else and it was time for us to part ways. He didn't give up easily. Every night when I would return from a date with Justin, Brad was always at my front door asking for just one more night together. Knowing that if I was seriously going to pursue a meaningful relationship with Justin, I had no choice but to turn Brad away. Eventually the front porch was void when I got home from seeing Justin, and Brad returned to his former lover.

After a few dates, Justin decided that it was time for me to come to his house for dinner. I gladly accepted the invitation and eagerly awaited the time to come.

When I pulled in to Justin's driveway that evening I was delighted with what I saw. He had a charming house and everything seemed to be well maintained. The house presented itself in such a way that there was no mistake that the person dwelling within it was a person with a great deal of pride, and that had always been very important to me.

When Justin opened the door to greet me, my first thought was, "He looks very different". Up until that point I had only seen him in a business suit as we always met right after he got out of work. Tonight he was wearing a light blue polo shirt that brought out the beautiful blue in his eyes, and a pair of khaki shorts that allowed me to see what playing basketball for many years could do for one's legs.

After he kissed me on the cheek and welcomed me in, he turned to go to the kitchen to open the bottle of wine I had brought for the evening. It was then that all I could do was admire his strong calf muscles that flexed with every step he made as he walked away from me towards the kitchen.

Soft music was playing in the background. With only the sound of an acoustic piano coming from the stereo and a room lit only by the flames of dozens of candles, I was sure this was going to be a night I would never forget. And that is indeed what it became.

After dinner, Justin and I went into his sunroom to finish our wine and just as we were about to kiss, there was a knock on the front door. When Justin opened the front door to reveal a girl standing there offering him a house plant, his countenance immediately changed. The look on his face was like he had been caught peeing in someone's iced tea.

Instantly I knew that this wasn't just a friendly visit and Justin seemed quite irritated with the unannounced visitor. So was I. As she handed him the plant and kissed him right on the lips, I knew there was more to this story than I thought and began to think of how I was going to deal with this blonde and busty bitch.

She was introduced as Lorna and I was introduced as a buddy that was over for a few drinks. When she saw the candles that were the only light in the room and noticed the soft music, she was fully aware that I wasn't over to kick back and watch the game.

Lorna didn't stay but for a short while but it seemed like an eternity. After she left, I asked Justin just what that was all about and he proceeded to tell me that he had dated her for a while after he moved to Atlanta and she just wasn't willing to let him go. I told him that this night may help her to loosen the leash a little bit.

Being from a small town in Kentucky, Justin had fought many of the same demons that I had and he had tried very hard not to be gay. He had been on the basketball team and being a big sissy just didn't fit that profile. That was what gave him the legs that I couldn't keep my eyes off of.

The rest of the night didn't turn out as Justin and I had hoped that it would. The uninvited guest seemed to consume the conversation for the rest of the evening as Justin began to worry about what Lorna would have to say at work the following day. He was quite sure that she would out him to their co-workers and he worried that the result of that would ultimately be the beginning of the end of the career that he had worked so diligently to obtain.

After about an hour of worrying and bitching, I decided that it was time for me to retire for the evening and announced that I should be leaving. At this point, Justin turned to me and said, "Please stay. I can deal with work tomorrow. Tonight I want only you." so I decided to stay with him that night.

The night was very tender, just as I expected it to be. A gentleman that greets you at the door is, most often, a gentleman in the bedroom. When I looked up to see his eyes I was pleasantly surprised to see that they weren't closed. His eyes were watching me the entire time. He wanted to please me. That was something that hadn't happened in a very long time. Most of the men that I had been with up until this point seemed interested in only their pleasure. That wasn't the case with Justin. He wanted to please me and it was obvious. During the final measure of our intimate rhapsody, I knew that this would not be the last time I knew this pleasure. Perhaps this would be a lifetime…I was in love.

The morning arrived and I remember thinking, "Is my scar showing? My hair must be a mess! My God! I can smell my own breath!". To my relief, Justin was already out of the bed, showered, completely dressed in his suit and was down the hall cooking breakfast. Coffee had never smelled as good as it did that morning. I couldn't wait to get to the end of the hallway and participate in that morning ritual and I can remember thinking that I wanted every morning that I had left on this earth to be just like that one.

As I turned the corner and entered the kitchen, Justin was standing there with a fresh magnolia bloom in his hand that he had gone out and picked just for me and as he handed it to me, he pronounced his love for me and asked me if I would like to move in with him. Those were the most exciting words I had ever heard in my entire life before I had breakfast. Without pause, I jumped into his arms and shouted, "Yes! I have been in love with you since the first time I saw you!". His response was quick, as he announced that he, too had fallen for me in a very short time.

The next few days were the most exciting I had known for a very long time. I was preparing to move in with the man that I just knew was to be the love of my life. Justin was dealing with rumors at work and trying to stomp out the fires that were burning his reputation and status as the proverbial stud on campus.

It was a different world at my place of employment. People were actually excited for me. Even the straight burly manager, the black Baptist lady that washed dishes, the straight female waitresses that were jealous of my stud, and even the closet case bar keep (that I was sure would come out of the closet as soon as he heard my news) were sincerely interested in hearing all of the details. I was happy…and other people were happy for me. At the time I couldn't imagine life being any better than it was right then.

The day for Justin hadn't been quite as encouraging as mine. As I pulled into his driveway that evening with the first of many things to incorporate into his home, he seemed to be having mixed emotions. He assured me that he was thrilled that I was moving in with him and that he had no greater desire, but he was concerned with the way that he was now being shunned at work. The news of the previous night had traveled quickly throughout the office where Justin worked and it wasn't received as well in his world as it was in mine. In Justin's world, he was now the worst of the worst…he was a leper.

Somehow, overnight, he had developed an incurable disease and it may be contagious!

Justin was amazed at the way he was now being treated at work. Prior to the rumors, he had been the one that everyone wanted to be with after work, the popular guy…the one with all the answers and the one that could solve any problem no matter how big or small. Now he was the one with the problem. And it was a problem that couldn't be washed off.

The next few weeks weren't easy for Justin as the rumors and laughing behind his back continued. The days grew very long for him and fear and doubts of being fired began to consume him. When he came home at night, beaten down by his betrayers, I did my best to console him and assure him that things would get better, and eventually they did.

Mama Rosa, as she was called at work, began to ask Justin to join her and some of her friends for lunch. It took several attempts on Mama Rosa's part to convince Justin, but eventually he went along.

The day Justin went with his new friend was a turning point in his life. When he came through the door that night I knew that something was different. For the first time in several months, Justin's eyes were sparkling again and he was almost giddy with laughter. After I asked him what had happened, he took me in his arms and swung me around in a ballroom twirl and told me that he actually had new friends at work and that some of them may actually be gay! He was elated at the prospect of having others around him for support and camaraderie. We poured ourselves a couple of scotch and waters and danced in the living room for the rest of the night.

The next day was a Saturday and we decided to take a picnic to Piedmont Park and sit and enjoy the beautiful new day. The park was bustling with people and dogs as it was the first really nice day of Spring that year. The leaves were budding on the trees and the dogwoods had just begun to bloom. It was almost as if Mother Nature had sent a message to Justin telling him that he had a brand new world to enjoy living in.

As we nearly reached our picnic destination, Justin stopped dead in his tracks and the color drained from his face as he exclaimed, "Shit!" Not knowing whether to duck to dodge an oncoming meteor or to run from a maddened dog, I froze as well and asked what the matter was. It was at that moment when one of the two girls headed directly towards us screamed Justin's name.

Jeanne was a girl that Justin worked with and he had no idea as to how she would receive him after the news of him being gay had spread around the workplace as it had. Within an instant, all fears were relieved as Jeanne introduced us to her girlfriend, Connie.

After we spent the rest of the day with Jeanne and Connie, Justin was even more excited to find out that they lived just around the corner from us and were more than eager to have us over for dinner.

Jeanne, Connie, Justin and I became very close friends and before long, we were just like a family. There was hardly a night that either they were at our house, or we were at theirs. Eventually we began to take vacations together and shared all of our deepest secrets with one another.

Finally, the time came for Justin's parents to make their first visit to Atlanta since Justin and I had become a couple. This would prove to be a tiring experience, as Justin's parents had no idea that he was gay which resulted in the troubles of setting up one of the extra bedrooms so that it appeared to be where I stayed.

The parents finally arrived and Justin and I were more nervous than a couple of long-tailed cats in a room full of rocking chairs. The greetings were cordial and everything seemed to be going as planned thus far. We all enjoyed a nice dinner on the back patio and several inquiries were made as to the whereabouts of Lorna. Every time that name was mentioned I could see Justin tense up as he exhausted every mental energy to pull another lie out of thin air.

Finally, everyone grew weary and we all retired to our rooms for the night. The next morning was just as common as any other as we all sat around the breakfast table to discuss the plans for the day. Having no idea what to do with these people who were now my in-laws (without them having any knowledge of it), I had decided to remove myself from the situation and pick up a couple of extra shifts at work. What happened while I was mindlessly waiting tables was a very unexpected turn of events.

Justin's Father had decided to stay at the house and read the paper while Justin and his mom went to Home Depot to pick up some things for a project that Justin and his father had planned to work on that day.

The ride to Home Depot that morning ended up having a lasting impact on the rest of Justin's life. It incidentally became the exact moment when Justin accidentally came out to his mother. As they were riding along, Justin had a sudden mental vacation from reality and began to say to his mother, "While we're at Home Depot, I want to look at ceiling fans. Banjo and I need one in our bedroom." The words were still suspended in the air and Justin hit the brakes and pulled the car off to the side of the road before the inevitable question would be released from his mother's lips.

When I got home from work that night I immediately sensed the tension in the room as Justin pulled me aside and said, "We need to talk". With that, I knew that something wasn't good. It had been my experience that those words were usually followed by, "I need my space" or "This just isn't working out". With the thoughts of packing my bags and moving on thundering through my head, I followed Justin out to the back porch.

When the tears started flowing from Justin's eyes and he grabbed me and hugged me like he never had before, I started thinking that maybe a U-Haul wasn't necessarily in my near future. Then he told me what had happened. My body went numb and I broke out into a cold sweat. Especially after he told me that his father also knew at this point. (Apparently I had missed quite a day!) My initial response was to run as I screamed, "Are you fucking kidding me?! Your Father carries a gun!" My imagination went wild. I could only visualize Justin's

Father pretending to be okay with the occurrences of the day only to wait patiently for my arrival to put a bullet through my head and tell me I had ruined his son.

After Justin assured me that everything was okay and that he and his parents had settled all doubts and confusion during the day, he let go of my body that was still trying to flee from the future crime scene that I had envisioned in my head. We then headed inside to the house that was so eerily silent, as his parents had decided to take an early slumber.

The next day arrived and I couldn't wait to get out of the house and on to work. The usual "Good mornings" were delivered and I was on the way out the door. This day would be a day that I would regret for years to come.

After explaining to one of my good friends at work that day what had happened the day before, her suggestion was that the two of us should smoke a fat joint before I returned to the stressful situation that awaited me at home. As soon as our shift ended, we headed to her house to smoke.

Anita and I went straight from work to her apartment where her boyfriend had rolled and left a joint the size of conduit and left it on the coffee table for her. The second she lit it up, I knew that it was probably a bad idea, but decided I needed to calm down before I returned home to deal with whatever had transpired there while I was gone.

As soon as the last of the smoke cleared the air, I began my journey home. My head was spinning with the thoughts of how terrible it could be when I reached my destination that, not long ago, seemed to be a haven from the bitter and cruel world. Buford Highway seemed to be the best bet for me to get home safely since I was already dealing with the paranoia of the joint I had just shared with Anita.

The traffic light seemed to stay red much longer than it ever had before as I sat there waiting and discussing with myself how to handle the situation that awaited me at home. Then, out of the blue, there was the screeching of tires sliding across asphalt and the sounds of metal crunching and glass shattering. The next thing I knew, a helpless body flew through the air directly in front of my car and landed, lifeless and limp, only ten feet away from my car.

After I dialed 911 and stepped on the gas, my life began to close in around me. The thoughts of that breathless person lying on the cold asphalt made my mind begin to race. The thoughts of the possibility of that being me and wondering when the word would be delivered to the people that love me began to consume my every thought. On that drive home, the world became very real to me. What if that had of been Justin just a week ago? His parents would have never been able to realize the real person that they had loved for all of those years. Suddenly, the announcement of who he was in love with probably wouldn't have seemed to be such a big deal after all. Then I began to think of the dead lady in the street and I said a prayer for her in hopes that all of her life was in order. I hoped that if there was a similar circumstance in her life, that she had dealt with it before it was too late.

When I arrived at the place that I now knew as home, the place where I could take refuge from the world outside, I sat in my car and wondered: "What would happen if I just simply went inside and kissed my boyfriend and told him I love him right in front of his parents?" Several minutes went by as I sat in my car and waited for the rest of the buzz of the marijuana to subside. With tears in my eyes, I summoned up the strength to go inside the house and pretend like the issues that Justin's family was dealing with were the most important in the world. Meanwhile, a lady was dead in the street and her family didn't know where she was.

The time came for Justin's parents to pack up and head back to Kentucky. It was an emotional morning and many tears were shed. The thoughts that were weighing heavily on everyone's mind was the hopes that this would not be the end of life as they knew it. Hopefully love would prevail and everyone would find their way to peace through it.

As Justin and I stood in the street and waved goodbye until his parents were out of sight, I realized that I had found a special person to share my life with. As tears rolled down his cheek and he held my hand, I rested comfortably in that moment and trusted that everything would work out for the best.

It took several phone calls for Justin's mom to finally say that she could actually deal with him being gay, but the hard part was for her to actually think about him with another man. Justin's father, on the other hand, seemed to be dealing with it just fine. He even asked questions about me. He wanted to know how I was, how my family was, and was inquisitive as to how my family dealt with the situation.

Justin and I had been to see my family on several occasions prior to the last scene. The first time was slightly uncomfortable as Justin was the first boyfriend that I had taken to my family's home since Sean and I had broken up a couple of years earlier.

My father, who was still an active member in the Baptist church had taken to Justin immediately. The two of them had many things in common. Justin was, seemingly, the idea of a son that my father had in mind when I was born. He was athletic, loved to fish, and was interested in listening to all of the stories that my father had to tell. My father got to the point where he would sometimes hug Justin before me when we would arrive. That thrilled me. The thought that a man that was born in 1918, who was brought up to think that it was perfectly fine to think that people of a different race were to be subordinate to him, was actually hugging my boyfriend and welcoming him into our family home was something I thought I would never see in my lifetime.

It seemed that it was just days earlier when things were much different in my home. One episode that changed the dynamics of my life with my father had occurred in the very room where he was now embracing my boyfriend.

It had been a wonderful night with us sitting around after dinner and having a glass of wine when the proverbial shit hit the fan. The conversation was going rather well and my father began to tell the story of how his mother used to feed the colored folk from their back porch after his father had gone off to work. Realizing that my father meant no harm by the expression that he was about to release into the universe, I decided to jump up in the middle of the floor and scream to the top of my lungs, "GOD DAMN IT" as soon as the word nigger was announced. It amazes me to this day that I didn't get thrown over his knee and felt the thrash of his belt against my naked ass at that point but, fortunately, I had the element of surprise in my court.

With one look from my father, I knew that I must immediately go into a deep and thorough explanation of my outburst. As it turned out, my father was much more receptive to rationalization than I had given him credit for. With a simple explanation that his "N" word was as offensive to me

74

as my "GD" was to a good Baptist, no further explanation was needed. That was the last time I heard my father use that term, and out of respect for him, that was the last time I used the name of his God in vain.

As time went on, Justin and I would visit my family more and more often and they would drive down to Atlanta to visit with us in our home for extended weekends. Eventually, Jeanne and Connie became regular fixtures at our family gatherings and before long, we all learned to love each other and enjoy being around each other and we developed a love that is difficult to come by, unless everyone involved is willing to let their guard down and experience the life of another culture.

As time progressed, It never ceased to amaze me how my father enjoyed my friends. A Baptist Deacon just wasn't supposed to associate himself with known lesbians and gay men. Fortunately, my Father didn't listen to doctrine as much as he listened to his own heart. He was taught to love, and he did it whole heartedly.

It seemed that Justin and I had found each other at the right time in each of our lives. It was a time that we both were transitioning from lives of lies to a world of truth. We grew alongside each other and supported one another with the trials that we both dealt with regarding what the world seemed to measure us by. Our sexuality seemed to be the one thing that people outside of our circle couldn't get past. We were always invited to parties and were more often than not, the life of those parties. But when the party was over, we were still the token queers.

One afternoon while I was shopping at Lenox Square, I ran into Kirsten. I couldn't believe my eyes! There she was, looking just as she did the last day I saw her at the Winston-

Salem School of the Arts the morning after I had slept with her black male classmate! The confrontation was unavoidable, yet I still wanted to run for the door because I knew that I had hurt her and wasn't ready to hone up to the past.

Her smile was as sweet and welcoming as if nothing had ever happened and she hugged me and said we should have a drink…immediately! So we headed for the nearest restaurant and bellied up to the bar.

It was during the next few hours that I began to realize that life was a gigantic puzzle and I was better off not trying to force the pieces into place. Obviously things worked out better when the picture was put together by the great artist of the universe.

Over a dozen drinks, Kirsten told me that she had absolutely no harsh feelings towards me and that she completely understood what I had been going through at the time. She was devastated, but after a long talk with her parents, she knew that it wasn't easy for me to be honest with her. Her parents had told her that they knew I was gay all the while, but they thought it best for her to realize these things on her own. They had been through the coming out process with their son, and knew full-well what I was going through. Again, I thought, what amazing people!

Kirsten and I resumed our friendship as if nothing had ever happened and she told me that she was singing in a local lounge that night and that I should go home and get Justin and bring him along to hear her perform.

Kirsten still sounded like an angel to me and Justin couldn't believe her talents either and the three of us became the best of friends. We became such good friends that she moved in with us for several months after one of her relationships went sour.

It wasn't long until Kristen grew tired of the Atlanta scene and decided that it was time to move on so she packed her bags and set off for Los Angeles in pursuit of a singing career. Her ambition was tremendous to me. The thoughts of simply saying, "Screw it" and packing up and leaving were so romantic to me. But there was no way I could be that far away from my family. Fear stood in my way and she ran it over as she peeled out of the driveway with a back pack, a guitar and a dream.

Justin's job was going well and I had recently taken a position at a country club in a very prestigious area of Atlanta which kept me away from home most evenings and weekends.

Working in a country club can be rather challenging if you know that you don't suit the opinions of the membership as to what a good citizen of the community is. Therefore: Gay equals controversy and that is one thing the socialites of Atlanta simply will not tolerate in their glass house of socialization. Fortunately, what the socialites don't realize is what goes on behind the service doors.

Liezel was the lady who interviewed me for the position and I was mesmerized by her from the very moment I met her. She was from Liverpool and when she spoke it was all I could do to understand a word that came out of her mouth and I couldn't wait to know what she was saying and listen to every story that I could summon from her memory of what I was sure to be a fantastic life. Her accent was very heavy and unlike any I had ever heard before.

Liezel and I became very good friends and after she was introduced to Justin, Jeanne and Connie, she immediately became a part of our family. And she became my rock when things got rough at work. Sometimes I was asked to fill in for different positions at the club during the absence of a worker at the pro shop or the Men's Grill. Those times were tough for me as I had no knowledge of how to speak the language of the jocks who frequented those restricted areas of the club. When I became the brunt of the jokes of the men who spent their free time there, Liezel was always there to comfort me and make sure I left for the day with a laugh.

The Men's Grill at the club was an extremely mysterious place to me. It was in the lower section of the massive building and it always smelled of musky golf shoes and cigars. What drew the men to that place was a mystery to me. The space was adorned with the finest appointments. Dark, rich woods lined the walls and bars, and the carpets were a luxurious hunter green. It was a fine looking place, but the secrecy of it was confusing to me. I couldn't figure out why the men who frequented the place laughed at me for wanting the company of men, but they spent thousands of dollars a year to be in the absence of women. Often times I wanted to tell them that I knew of several places that they could accomplish the same goal for a small five dollar cover charge. Liezel helped me to look on the less serious side of the Men's Grill and the laughter that was inside me each time I had to work there seemed to sustain me.

My new family of trusted friends continued to grow closer and closer and then one day Justin came home with some astounding news: He was being transferred to Los Angeles. The news came as a shock to me but I felt that I had no choice but to go with him since I had committed my life to him. My love for him was so strong that I could not imagine my life without him. I also realized that I would no longer be able to drive to North Carolina just to have lunch with my mom, dad and sister.

The day that I went to tell my family that I was going to be moving to California was a difficult one. The sadness of knowing that I would be so far away from my strongest support group was overwhelming, but there was a sense of excitement about being on the west coast with Justin.

When I arrived at my parents home they were both waiting expectedly as I had told them I had big news. We sat in the living room and chatted about our daily lives for a while until my mother asked what the big news was. After I announced that I would be moving to California with Justin, the tears began to flow. None of us were prepared to be that far away from each other. An hour later, we regained our composure and started talking about the opportunities we would have: They could go and revisit some of the places they saw on their honeymoon, we could take road trips to the wine country, and we could even drive out to Vegas if we wanted to. All of those were empty words as we knew that a great geographical distance was a couple of months away from disturbing the life that we had for so long taken for granted.

When I got back to Atlanta, I immediately turned in my notice at the country club and was prepared to pack up my life and move it across the country. That night as I lay in bed next to Justin, half of me was filled with excitement thinking about our journey, and the other half was filled with dread because I knew it would be months before I could see my family again.

Exactly one week before Justin and I were to make our move to California, we had gone to bed and everything seemed to be on track. We had been asleep for a couple of hours and precisely at two o'clock in the morning, I sat straight up in bed and was trembling. The bed was shaking so vigorously from my tremors that it woke Justin up and he asked me what was the matter. Without a pause I told him that I couldn't go to California with him. Instantly, a mix of anger and sadness overtook him. To this day, I don't know what awakened me in the middle of the night with that revelation and I may never know. I can only trust that there was a reason for it and one day I will know…and Justin will know. ~

People enter our lives everyday and none of them are without reason. Every time a person smiles at you, there is potential for a friendship. If you don't smile back, you are forfeiting that opportunity. You may be an executive in a high profile company and dismiss the smile that the lady in the company cafeteria sends your way and miss a great opportunity to learn how better to cut the cost of paper cups in the company cafeteria. You may be the lady in the company cafeteria and dismiss the smile that the CEO sends you and miss the opportunity to hear about the new position in the public relations office. Or you may just miss the opportunity to make a great friend. Either way, it's tragic not to pay attention to and care for those around you whether you know them or not. When you learn to listen with your heart and follow the lead of your instincts, you will usually find yourself in a place of great content. To have true friends is one of life's greatest blessings. But you can't always be on the mountain top. Once in a while you have to go back to the valley to appreciate the great mountain. Every once in a while you just have to EXPECT…

Chapter Seven
"Confusion"

——⟨⟨⟨⟩⟩⟩——

**(An act or instance of confusing. The
quality or state of being confused)**

O ften in life, certain circumstances occur that leave
you with a sense of bewilderment and the feeling of
being completely lost. Those moments become the axis of
confusion and can begin to spin your world into complete and
utter chaos. These are the times to expect your life to change
drastically. To realize that change is good is to open your eyes
and realize that there is a master plan for your life and it is up
to you to follow the lead of the spirit that lives inside of you.
The changes that occur in life often seem to lead to a dark and
lonely place but if you follow your heart, you will find the old
adage to be true: It is darkest just before the dawn.

——⟨⟨⟨⟩⟩⟩——

~ The morning after my revelation was an eye-opening experience that I hadn't had a chance to prepare myself for. Justin was a different person. He was angry, and with justifiable reason. Announcing the news that I would not be accompanying him on his new quest in life didn't sit well with him; especially since there was now less than one week to pack up the house and head across the country.

It was a fortunate coincidence that one of the girls that worked at the country club with me was also in search of a place to live. Her father was also being transferred out of the state of Georgia and she had decided to stay in Atlanta. So it was agreed that Sarah and I would become roommates.

Sarah was a vibrant and beautiful girl. Her long brown hair was always brushed and in perfect coif. She and I had been friends for several months at this point and we knew that we would get along swimmingly as roommates. We instantly began referring to ourselves as Will and Grace.

Sarah and I found a place quickly and began setting up our new home within a couple of days and were adjusting to our new lives. The apartment we found was perfect. It was just around the corner from our jobs. There was a nice sized living room, kitchen and dining area in the middle of the apartment, and we each had our own bedrooms and bathrooms on opposite sides of the communal area.

Justin and I had decided that if anyone could make a long distance relationship work it was surely the two of us. We stayed together until his last night in Georgia and the morning of his departure came quickly. That afternoon he dropped me off at the apartment and we had our final kiss just before he drove off. Just then it hit me. I had no idea what was going to happen to me next and I found myself feeling very alone and frightened. As soon as Justin's car was out of sight, I ran upstairs and into my bedroom, where I threw myself onto my bed and sobbed for hours. My only thoughts were, "Have I just made the biggest mistake of my life? What will I do now?" Knowing that it is more than far-fetched to really make a long-distance relationship work, I felt a deep depression start to settle in. Then it was my new confidant, Sarah, that came to the rescue. She laid down beside me and held me in her arms and reassured me that Justin and I still shared the same love that we always had and that California was only a four hour flight away. After the tears stopped flowing, we opened a bottle of wine and made a toast to new beginnings.

Life at the country club remained much the same and work was the only sense of security I felt that I had at the time. All of my new friends were at the club and we all soon began going out together and the empty hole in my spirit was soon mostly filled with the family I had at work.

Liezel and I found ourselves in a very meaningful and strong friendship. There was nothing I couldn't share with her and she was always more than happy to listen to me. Eventually we started heading downtown to the gay bars almost every night after work and Justin was growing suspicious of what I was up to when he would call the apartment and find that I was rarely home.

There was a bar in mid-town called the Armory and that was where Liezel and I would end up most nights. It was a gay paradise. Just about any night of the week the bar was filled to capacity with beautiful men and soon my eyes began to wander and I found myself in the beds of many of what the Armory had to offer me. Eventually I began to realize that my biggest problem was that I couldn't stand being alone, and I certainly couldn't stand sleeping alone. The fact that I had no idea who half of the men were that I woke up next to didn't matter as much as the fact that I was beginning not to be able to recognize myself either…for a short while.

One night's journey to the Armory led to the beginning of the road that would change my life forever. It would later prove to be a long and winding road, but a road worth traveling down. ⁓

Confusion is a large part of any life changing decision. It is the root of doubts that swarm the conscious and unconscious mind when making the important decisions in life. Sometimes you know exactly what the right decision is. Sometimes the answers just aren't that clear. The decisions that hold the power to change your life are the decisions that seem the most challenging to figure out. The results of those decisions are sometimes seen instantly, sometimes they are realized a little later on and some of the repercussions are never fully realized.

There is a calm assurance that can be found just after a decision has been made that has been a struggle to deal with. Even if you don't know right away whether or not you made the right decision, the burden of making the decision is immediately relinquished. That is the moment when you begin to move forward and design your life based on the outcome of your decision.

When the confusion of right or wrong has been dealt with, and it must be dealt with, it is time to jump from the cliff and EXPECT…

Chapter Eight
"Excitement"

(A feeling of great enthusiasm and eagerness)

E xcitement is most often associated with the expectation that something wonderful is about to happen. Usually the thing that you're most excited about consumes your every thought. The excitement of a first date can result in a non-productive day at work or school. With thoughts of what to wear, where to go, and "Will he kiss me?" ringing in your head. During the time leading up to the event, it is difficult to focus on anything else.

Excitement is usually linked to a joyous upcoming event and it usually devours the less desirable thoughts that were there prior to excitement's arrival. When some event or occurrence holds the capacity to change your life and bring you the joy that you have long searched for, it is impossible not to immerse yourself into the immense feelings that are associated with it. Those times are rare, savor every moment of them.

~~~~~

~ July thirty-first started off just as any other day: Wake up with a hangover, take two aspirin, get dressed and rush off to work. It was an uneventful day and by day's end, I realized that I needed to do something to spice it up so I called some of my bar-hopping friends and organized a night on the town.

The last stop of the night would be at the Armory. My friends and I had decided that since we were already out, we might as well make a night out of it and head for the dance club.

The bar was bursting at the seams with men. It was definitely going to be a good night. Just how good, I would realize a few short minutes later.

The bar was organized in such a way that everything revolved around the actual bar itself, and there was a steady flow of people around the bar that formed a two-way traffic pattern which resulted in a plethora of men to gaze upon and flirt with as they passed by.

The second lap around the bar would result in an experience that would last in my mind as one of the fondest memories of my entire lifetime.

As I was walking around the bar holding on tightly to my beer, I looked up and saw the most handsome man looking right back at me. There were about three people between himself and me and I felt my entire body tense up as I waited for the crowd to push us closer together. When he was right next to me and smiling with a smile that darkened the rest of the room, I lost the ability to think or speak and some strange force overtook my body. Before I knew what I was doing, I simply reached out and patted him on the stomach and continued on to the next lap as I turned to see a complete look of confusion written across his beautiful face.

During the next run around the bar my thoughts were consumed with the thoughts of what would I say to him on the next round. I had to think of something and I had to think of it fast. It was as if there was no one else in the bar for the next ten minutes that it took me to reach him again. He was all I could think about.

When I looked up and saw him coming, my brain was suddenly void of all thoughts once again. Fortunately, he had been thinking during the last round as well and had managed to think of something to say: "Hi, I'm Tomas". It must have been a few seconds before my neurons started firing again as I just stood there smiling like a dumb beast.

Tomas was the most intriguing person I had ever found roaming the bars in Atlanta and I knew that I needed to come up with a game plan quickly. As he stood before me it was all I could do to form a complete sentence. His hair was jet black and he had the thickest and most luscious eyebrows and eyelashes that perfectly framed his dazzling blue eyes. He was gorgeous and I had to have him.

The conversation was awkward as I was still searching for something interesting to say. When he asked me what sports I liked to play I really started to freak. My initial thought was, "Sports? Are you kidding me? What the hell kind of a question is that in a gay bar? Maybe his brain has gone numb, too!" In case this turned out to be a legitimate question, I shouted out the first sport that came to mind: "Tennis!" Even though it had been several years since I had swung a tennis racquet, I thought maybe I could at least carry on a conversation for at least twenty seconds about it.

Fortunately, Tomas was more interested in dancing than talking and he asked me to join him on the dance floor.

For whatever reason, my brain, again, went in another direction. Instead of following Tomas to the dance floor, I headed towards the bar where I ordered another beer.

A few seconds later I felt a tap on my shoulder and Tomas was standing behind me with a rather perplexed look on his face. "I thought you wanted to dance." he asked me. My responses kept getting more and more moronic. What I said even surprised me. "Oh, you meant now?" I'm sure he must have been thinking, "No, you dumb ass. I meant November first." He seemed very patient with me and led me to the dance floor where we danced for a good hour. After that, we headed back to the bar and my courage had begun to return and I asked him if he would like to go home with me the following night. His response was a complete surprise to me as he quickly said, "Tomorrow? What's wrong with tonight?". I told him that I was there with a few friends but I would more than happily bail on them and that I just needed a few minutes to tell them that they needed to find someone to hook up with that night because I had driven and they would need wheels out of town.

When I returned to Tomas he was ready to go so I led him out to my car. The little red Miata seemed to impress him and I hoped it would eventually make up for the lie I had told him about playing tennis if it ever came up again. Thank God I hadn't said football, as I knew absolutely nothing about that sport.

After I threw the top back on the Miata, we were on our way. We hadn't gotten more than a mile away from the bar when I turned to look at Tomas, and saw that his head was leaned back against the head rest and he was sound asleep. That surprised me and worried me at first but then I thought it may be a good idea that he got the rest while he could as I had big plans for him for the rest of the night. Just as I was finishing with that thought, I heard an explosion and turned to look at the road and discovered that we were air-born. During my brief gaze at the sleeping stud, I had hit a curb, blown a tire and was now headed straight for a telephone pole.

A quick turn of the wheel saved us from an early demise and I was now faced with the task of getting back to a gas station and calling AAA to come and change the tire.

We slowly made it back to safety and I dialed the number for AAA on my cell phone and they informed me that it could possibly be an hour and a half before they could get there. Not willing to risk Tomas losing interest and wanting to go home, I opened the trunk and began my search for a spare tire and what ever equipment might be necessary to improve our situation.

After a few head scratches and attempts at uncovering anything round with screw holes in it, I finally found the small tire and began to jack the car up and change the tire myself. It would be several months later that Tomas would inform me that was the precise moment he knew I was the one. He was quite impressed with the fact that I could change my own tire.

After the twenty minute fix-a-flat episode, we were back in the car and headed up the Eighty-Five towards my apartment. I couldn't wait to get this man home and see what the rest of the night had in store for me.

When we entered the apartment, I grabbed a couple of beers and led Tomas to my bedroom. Apparently there was no time for idle chit-chat and a drink. He was ready to rumble.

That night was the most exciting sexual experience I had ever had. Tomas had the perfect equipment and knew exactly what to do with it. He was a real man.

Actual sleep never occurred for me the rest of the night. After our raucous activities were over, all I could do was lie there and look at this spectacular man lying next to me with the moon light glowing on his silhouette.

When morning did arrive, I hoped that he wouldn't wake up. I wanted that moment to last forever. There had been many mornings when I woke up and would rather saw my own arm off than to wake the beast next to me, but this wasn't one of those mornings. I actually wanted to tie this one to the bed so that he could never leave. Some mornings consisted of me trying desperately to think of a reason to get whoever the hell that was that I slept with the night before out of my apartment. Tomas made me want to stay in bed all day and get to know the man that was under my sheets.

Reality always comes around and here it was. It was time for Tomas to go home and get ready for work, so I gave him my phone number and kissed him good-bye. With a promise to call me later, he was out the door and gone. Moments later, he knocked on the door and reminded me that I had driven him there and that he would need a ride back down town.

The rest of the day seemed like an eternity. The fear of missing Tomas's phone call kept me from doing anything outside of my apartment that day until it was time to go to work.

When I arrived at work, Sarah, who had been briefed that morning of the previous night's ordeal, was eagerly awaiting my arrival to ask if he had called or not. As my smile disappeared, I could only say, "No". She tried to convince me that he would but I had already begun to lose hopes of ever seeing my dreamy Tomas again.

That evening I called home to check the answering machine every ten minutes to see if my long awaited message was there. The twelfth machine check was the one that I had waited for. His voice was soft in the message and he told the machine what a wonderful time he had the night before and was looking forward to seeing me again. He left his number and asked for me to return his call.

When I got home that night, the first thing I did was to call Tomas and we made plans to meet the next night for dinner. My heart was in my throat. Those plans left me so full of excitement that I could hardly breathe. It had been a very long time since someone's voice made my knees go weak.

Sarah and Leizel had both expressed concerns regarding the fact that I was still involved with Justin and they both agreed and encouraged me to call Justin and discuss what was going on. I knew in my heart that calling Justin and telling him everything would be the best thing to do, but I was so afraid of hurting him that I let it go for a while.

The next day was filled with anxiety and excitement as I was getting ready for my first date with Tomas. We had plans to meet at a restaurant downtown and I could hardly wait to get there, but I didn't want to seem desperate and made sure that I would arrive fifteen minutes late. As it turned out, there was no traffic to speak of that night and I was actually five minutes early. So was Tomas. His first words were, "I'm so glad you were on time. My biggest pet peeve is for someone to be late.". Whew! Thank God there was no traffic!

Dinner wasn't to be without the element of surprise. Tomas informed me that we needed to talk. Those words are hardly ever followed with good news so I downed my drink and braced myself for the worst. The thoughts in my head began to swirl like a tornado in a trailer park. Did he have AIDS? Had he given me crabs? Was he in the witness protection program? What could it be?

The answer to my questions came quickly after. He was married! At that point I was wishing for the crabs.

Tomas began to explain his situation to me. He knew that he always had feelings for other men, but the only ones he ever saw in New Hampshire (where he was from) were ugly and he just couldn't see himself with any of them so he decided that he must not really be gay because he could find nothing in common with the gay men that he had encountered before.

After his transfer to Atlanta, he moved in to the area of the city called Mid-town, which is known to have a heavy population of gay people, and he soon found himself in the midst of men that were much more desirable to him and he had been going to the gay bars in the area and finding that he had quite a bit in common with these new and beautiful creatures.

Tomas had been in Atlanta for three months at this point and had made quite a few gay friends and had been on several dates with some of them. The night I met him was intended to be his last night of being gay.

When I inquired as to what he meant by it being his last night being gay, he told me that his wife and two children were on the way to Georgia in a U-Haul and would be arriving the next day, and that he had decided that he would have to go back in the closet and hide from himself once again. He then began to tell me that after he met me his feelings began to change and

92

that he would now be faced with a very difficult decision. Then he told me that I was the most unique person he had met and he had developed more than sexual desire for me.

We spent what I knew could have been our last night together and I kissed him good-bye the next morning wondering if I would ever hold him again.

When I got home the next morning and explained the situation to Sarah, she told me that he must be a horrible person to do that to his wife and that I should never talk to him again. I had different feelings about the latest development. There was a sadness in his eyes that morning when I left him and I wondered what it must be like to be living that lie. Having never met Tomas' wife, I already felt sorry for her. I wondered how many other women were going about their daily lives living with husbands who were in the same personal hell that Tomas was in. Then I began to think of how difficult it must be for Tomas. To want something and know that you could never have it and to hide behind an image that in no way reflected who he really was.

The next few days were anxious days. I was constantly wondering how the move-in was going, had the sparkle in Tomas' eyes diminished? Was he sleeping with her? The latter question seemed to bother me the most. The realization that I was the other woman didn't sit well with me and I found my self being something that I had never been before: jealous. It was a feeling that I knew wasn't right, he was her husband. For some reason that wasn't enough to keep me from thinking about him. I missed him, and I wanted to be with him.

A couple of days went by and my phone rang. It was Tomas! Just the sound of his voice made my heart race. He wanted to see me, and I wanted nothing more in the world.

We met at Piedmont Park that afternoon for a walk and it was the happiest I had been in days. He told me that he had missed me and was trying to figure out a way to be with me. It was the shortest hour I had ever experienced and it was time for him to go back to work.

Several hours after our departure from the park I received another unexpected call from Tomas. The reason for the call came as a complete shock. He wanted me to come over to his house that night and join him and his wife for dinner. After I regained consciousness I told him that I would be more than happy to join them for dinner. Having no idea what I was getting myself into, I decided that if he was up for the risk, who was I to piss against the wind?

Tomas had told his wife that he had made some new friends while he had been in Atlanta and that he would like for her to meet some of them. He told her that after dinner he and I would be joining some other friends for drinks and to watch a game.

As soon as I knocked on the door, I wanted to turn and run as fast as I could and never look back. I wanted to jump into my little Miata and put the gas pedal on the floor and race towards sanity. Where did I find the balls to put myself on those front steps?

Before my feet could take flight, the door opened and there she was. There had been some peculiar moments in my life prior to this one, but this moment was one that left me feeling like a person in a boxing match with no arms.

The woman that was Tomas' wife was standing before me and opening her front door for me to enter in. She had a sweet face that was embraced by brown, medium length dark brown hair. She was dressed in a common housewife wardrobe which consisted of a light blue cardigan, simple white pull-over shirt and a pair of khakis that I was sure came from wherever it was that suburban wives shop. Her words were kind and sweet as she introduced herself. "Hi, I'm Cassie. Tomas will be down in a moment, would you like a martini?" The Hallelujah Chorus went off in my head at the offering of a martini. My quick reply was a simple, "Yes, please".

Moments later Tomas joined us in the kitchen and I couldn't have been happier to see anyone in my entire life. I wanted to kiss him so badly but, instead, I was in the middle of giving Cassie her first reason to wonder why her husband had befriended me. Cassie, trying to make small talk with the stranger in her kitchen, had asked a simple question: "How has your week been?".

This particular week had been monumentally devastating to the gay community. Princess Diana had been killed in a car crash and Gianni Versace had been shot down on the front stairs of his South Beach home. Shortly after I expressed my deep sadness from those two events, Tomas jumped nervously in and started rattling off some kind of sports scores. Cassie simply looked puzzled. Her husband's new friend had been there for less than fifteen minutes and had already sucked down an entire martini. She then asked if I would like another one and I accepted the offer.

Shortly thereafter dinner was served. With two martinis already in me, and now holding a glass of wine, I began to relax. Somewhere in the middle of dinner, Cassie was speaking and I began to laugh. She wasn't telling a funny story, but my thoughts were entertaining me. As I looked across the table at Tomas and his wife, I thought that this must be the new version of "Guess Who's Coming to Dinner". It was difficult for me to look Cassie directly in the eyes so I never knew if she was amused or completely insulted by my behavior. With the fact that I had been sleeping with her husband, I realized that my silent entertainment was the least of the crimes committed and I complimented her on her culinary skills.

Dinner finally ended and it was time for Tomas and me to head out to watch the game with the boys. We didn't watch a game that night, but we were with the boys. The Armory was, once again, our destination.

Tomas and I would meet each day during his lunch hour and he would find ways to get out of the house to come and see me almost every night. Our affair lasted for a few weeks before things began to change.

One night after Sarah and I had finished washing the dishes and were polishing off a bottle of wine, the phone rang and it was Tomas. He sounded very anxious as he said that he needed to talk to me immediately.

As soon as I hung the phone up, I rushed straight out the door to meet Tomas at Cowtipper's again. He was outside in the parking lot waiting in his green Jeep Cherokee where I joined him. He had been crying and I instantly hugged him and asked what was wrong.

The news came as a huge surprise to me. He had told his wife that he was gay! I couldn't imagine what a difficult decision that must have been to make. It's hard enough coming out to your parents, but to basically tell a spouse that the last eight years of their life hadn't been at all as they thought must really be a total shit pot.

Not only had he told Cassie, but he had also been on the phone with his family for hours delivering the news to them as well. Tomas comes from a large Catholic family and at this point, they all seemed to handle it very well. His three sisters and two brothers offered nothing but support for him. His mother was a little surprised and his father was in absolute shock. When the shock wore off, denial set in for Tomas' father. Not denial that he had a gay son, but that he had a son at all. In one short moment Tomas no longer existed to his father.

When the crying ended, I took Tomas' hand and promised him that I would be there to support him through what was sure to be the toughest time of his life. He then raised my hand to his lips and kissed it and said, "I love you". ~

Excitement changes your entire body's chemistry. When the object of your desires finally calls, nothing else matters. Being overly enthusiastic about a new romance can truly make a fool out of you. It can cause you to laugh uncontrollably, jump up and down in the middle of a grocery store, or in some situations, cause you to forget where you are in life and thus, hurt other people around you.

There is always a feeling of exhaustion after the initial excitement begins to rescind and scientific evidence tells us that for every action there is an equal and opposite reaction. In some cases, after excitement ends, EXPECT…

Chapter Nine
"Bewilderment"

———∽∿∽———

(To be perplexed or confused)

Bewilderment can be a very powerful force. Sometimes in life you can be faced with choices that will ultimately effect the rest of your life. Oftentimes there are two choices to be made and both can be right, or both can be wrong. It is usually blind faith that leads you through these troubled waters and helps you to build a bridge to look down on the rivers of bewilderment and guide you down the right path.

Bewildering times should be viewed as times of learning. It shouldn't be feared, but revered. The decisions that you make during these times will offer up the final end to the situation and lead to the next stage of your life. Pay close attention to your heart and mind during bewilderment. The right decision is important and it will lead to your ultimate place of belonging.

~ After the shock of her husband coming out of the closet, Cassie decided to take their two children and move back to New Hampshire where she could seek refuge with her family and figure out her next move in life.

Tomas and I spent every second together that we possibly could and before we knew it, I was basically living with him. Sarah and her boyfriend were having problems that didn't seem to be manageable and she was preparing to move to Philadelphia to be with her family.

Justin had sensed long before that something was going on and had enlisted the help of our friends, Jeanne and Connie, to get to the bottom of it. I hadn't seen them in some time as I had been so deeply involved with Tomas and I assumed that their loyalty belonged to Justin anyway. Justin would call and Sarah would tell him I was out but would give me the message. Jeanne and Connie would drive by the apartment to find that my car was seldom there.

After Sarah moved and the apartment was abandoned, I was living with Tomas full time. Things shortly thereafter began to take some unusual turns.

With the freedom to be himself, Tomas was like an unleashed beast. He expressed his love for me, but also the curiosity of what all was out there. He would spend hours on the computer looking at images of other men and that didn't sit well with me at all. When I was growing up, the subject of sex was taboo in our home. It simply wasn't discussed. One night when my family was watching television, a couple began to get very intimate and my father lurched from his chair and kicked the television off. That's how sheltered from the subject we were and even twenty years later, I still wasn't comfortable talking about it or looking at pornographic images of it.

Relationships to me were between two people and that is all I was willing to accept. Finding Tomas on the computer late at night eventually started to upset me very deeply. With that, and new discussions about threesomes and other situations that I was very uncomfortable with began to drive my feelings and soon I began to wonder if I had made a mistake.

Justin and I still talked on occasion and one afternoon I was discussing with him what had developed with Tomas and he suggested that I fly out to California to visit him and explore our feelings and, if nothing else, find some form of closure to our relationship.

Not knowing how to discuss the situation with Tomas, I had told him that I was driving to North Carolina to visit my parents for a few days and my mother was asked to not reveal my whereabouts should he call there looking for me. Guilt was eating away at my soul but I had to figure out what was going on with my life and I needed to know if I had made the biggest mistake of my life.

When I arrived in Los Angeles, I was greeted by a very comforting and welcome smile. Justin seemed very happy to see me and I was equally glad to see him again.

The four days I was in California were very enlightening for both Justin and myself. Discussing what all had happened wasn't easy, but it was necessary. The biggest revelation that we got out of the trip was to find out that we really weren't as compatible in the bedroom as we should have been in order for our relationship to be a successful one. Over a scotch and water on the balcony one evening we had the courage to talk about sex and we discovered that we were both bottoms. That sure explained a lot. We loved each other dearly, but what we could have was true friendship. And that is what we had.

The next few days we had a great time together. Kirsten lived nearby and I was able to reconnect with her once again. The three of us spent the days on the beach and the evenings with their new friends. We laughed and cried a lot talking about the past and we all vowed to be friends forever.

When it was time for me to return to Georgia I was still filled with doubt. I loved Tomas, but I couldn't live under the circumstances of his curiosities. Some big decisions were still to be made.

When I rounded the corner into baggage claim back in Atlanta, I received yet another big surprise. Waiting at the carousel where my bag was to be retrieved was Tomas. His first words were, "The next time you go to North Carolina in January, you should pack a coat instead of a bathing suit". My heart was in my throat and words were not to be summoned. Having never been in a situation quite like this one, I had no idea what to say except, "I'm so sorry".

Not being aware of the moral misdemeanor that my mom and I had been participating in, my father had been the one to answer the phone when Tomas had called the house while my mother was in the shower. Apparently, the conversation went something like this: "Hi, Mr. Martini, is Banjo there?" My father's reply: "Well, no. He's in California."

When Tomas and I got back to the house that afternoon it was one of the most uncomfortable situations I had placed myself in to date. After the initial shock wore off, I was able to communicate once again and Tomas and I began to talk.

It wasn't going to be an easy thing to do, but after our talk, I decided that the best thing for me to do would be to move back to North Carolina until I could figure out what I was going to do next. Completely bewildered, I knew that to make the right decision, I needed to remove myself from the scene and look at it from another view. ~

When fear has subsided, change has occurred. After you realize who you are and have the courage and strength to live your life, true friends will help you muddle through the confusion. They will share your excitement and help you through the confusion and heartbreaking times because they see it in your eyes: You can EXPECT...

Chapter Ten

"Love"

———⟡⟡⟡———

**(Strong affection for another arising
out of kinship or personal ties)**

L ove is patient. Love is kind. Love is strong. Love is what
every soul searches for from birth until end of life. It
is the most valuable of all things on earth. Some spend an
eternity looking for it, and some times it was right beside them
the entire time, they just didn't open themselves up to it.

Love is a fierce warrior. Circumstances in life often
challenge the willpower and persistence of love's eternal fight,
but when there is love, it will win every time.

Love is the only emotion that can withstand a trial by
fire. All others burn and wither away, but true love comes out
sparkling.

When you find love, embrace it. Tend to it like the rarest of
all roses in the garden. It has stronger roots than any tree. It has

survived the floods of doubt, anger, and fear, and has emerged triumphant. Just like the other roses, it will bloom at certain times and at other times it will only show its foliage. When the fragrance fades for a while, nurture it and it will bloom again.

⁓ It was early in the morning when my sister and her husband arrived to help me load the U-Haul and head to North Carolina. The emotions were high and I was wondering if I was doing the right thing.

It was a long day but we finally got everything loaded and were ready to set off. Tomas pulled me aside and gave me a kiss good-bye and said that he hoped I could sort it all out and come back to him. He told me that he loved me and I climbed into the truck and I watched him, through a stream of tears, as he disappeared in the huge mirror on the side of the truck. At that moment I noticed the words that are on every other mirror on a vehicle and began to think, "maybe objects in mirror really are closer than they appear".

Moving back in with my parents after being out on my own for a while was often times challenging, but we needed and enjoyed the time together as we always had. Each night at dinner we would sit around and catch up on all that we had missed about being together all the time. It was a great bonding time for us. Each moment was treasured as none of us knew how long I was going to be there, or when I would set sail again. The future was so unclear to me at that point it was almost terrifying.

Each night I would receive phone calls from Tomas and Justin checking in to see how I was and to inquire as to what

I would be doing next. And every other day a fresh bouquet of roses would be delivered to me from Tomas.

Two weeks into my self-explorative sabbatical, the answer came clearly and sharply. During the middle of a relaxing bubble bath and a bottle of chardonnay, the phone rang and it was Tomas. He began to explain to me how much he missed me and how he loved me. When he said that he understood what I had been going through and forgave me for the trip to California that I was so dishonest to him about. I knew right then that anything that could survive a scenario like that must be true love.

The next morning over breakfast I broke the news to my parents. Now knowing that I truly loved Tomas, and that he truly loved me, I couldn't wait to get back to Atlanta and start the rest of my life with the man that I wanted to wake up to every morning for the rest of my life.

When Tomas called me that afternoon, I was already half-way to Atlanta and he had no idea. The plan was to surprise him; the hope was to not be surprised. When I asked him what he was doing that night, he said that he and his friend Trent were going to the Armory to renew their membership cards. At that point my plans were mapped out.

When Tomas and Trent walked through the doors of the Armory, I came out from behind a corner to greet them. The look on Tomas' face remains one of my favorite looks that I have ever seen on him. Without saying a word, he grabbed me and embraced me with a hug like I had never known. We both began to cry and he asked me if I was there to stay. "If you'll have me" was my reply. The answer was a definite yes and Trent began to cry as well, and said, "This is like a scene out of a Lifetime movie!".

Trent looked at Tomas and said, "Looks like you've got your ride home, I'll talk to you tomorrow" and he left. Tomas and I danced for most of the night. We danced like we had never danced before. Happiness and love had never seemed that close to me before and I didn't want that night to ever end. There wasn't a moment that our bodies weren't in contact on the dance floor, or when we returned home that night.

The divorce was settled quickly and amicably between Tomas and Carrie and now it was time for Tomas and me to start looking for our first house together.

After a brief search we found the perfect home in Lawrenceville, about an hour's drive outside downtown Atlanta. It was a quaint four bedroom home with an in-ground pool and it was all situated at the end of a cul-de-sac. It needed to be renovated, but we were up to the challenge and soon we began the project of making our new home perfect just for us.

Our neighborhood was five minutes away from Connie and Jeanne's house and I knew that it was inevitable that we would one day run into them. And that is exactly what happened. It was an ordinary shopping trip for groceries when I first saw Connie. We hadn't seen each other since my return from North Carolina and I wasn't sure if they would be angry with me for going back to Tomas.

Within seconds, Connie's arms were around me as she was telling me how great it was to see me and that she couldn't wait to meet Tomas. Being very relieved with her response, I couldn't wait to tell her how wonderful he was and that I couldn't wait for her and Jeanne to meet him.

A few nights later, Tomas and I had Connie and Jeanne over to have drinks by the pool. Almost instantly we were all inseparable and we were together almost every night either at our house or theirs.

When Tomas and I had nearly finished remodeling the house, we decided that it was time for a vacation. Connie and Jeanne were heading out for Florida in a few days and we asked it they minded if we joined them there. Of course they were thrilled by the idea, and that was our plan. They had forgotten to mention one major detail.

After Tomas and I checked into our hotel, we set off to find Connie and Jeanne. They were staying in a condo not far from where we were. We found their place and gently knocked on the door as it was early in the morning. When the door opened, the color drained from my face and once again, I found myself to be utterly speechless.

Connie and Jeanne had failed to mention the fact that Justin had moved back to Atlanta and would be in Florida the same time we were to be there. When the door opened and I looked up, it was Justin who was standing there. To say the moment was awkward would be like saying it wasn't a good idea for Ellen Degeneres and Anne Heche to get together.

After the first few seconds of complete silence passed, Justin simply said, "Come on in, boys". It was extremely uncomfortable at first, but after the first twelve-pack of Miller Lights had been consumed, the ill-at-ease moments disappeared and we all began to laugh at the situation.

As time went on, Connie, Jeanne, Justin and Liezel became our best friends and we became each others support group. After all that we had been through, we all agreed that we had so much invested in each other that nothing would do but for us to remain friends.~

Love is very forgiving. It exists in many forms. There is the love that you have for the one single person that simply takes your breath away. There is the kind of love that is reserved for very few people in your life. A true friend is rare and if you find just a few to share that form of love with, cherish them. Always tell them that you love them and always forgive them. At some point you may need to be forgiven as well.

After you have found that one special person to spend your life with, the one that gives you breath to face each new day, EXPECT...

Chapter Eleven
"Bliss"

(Complete Happiness)

Bliss is what happens when absolute joy overcomes simple happiness. Bliss is like the chocolate silk cake that follows the perfect birthday dinner; it is the Bailey's to the coffee.

Bliss is like the perfect finish to the best sex you ever had: the toe curling moment when the world erupts inside of you. It would be impossible to live every moment of your life in such pure ecstasy as your body would be in a constant tremor. Moments of bliss are the moments that add up to be the best memories of your life and they are the moments to be savored and enjoyed for they are rare.

~ It was on a warm Spring evening as Tomas and I were sitting around our pool enjoying the sounds and fragrances of the new season. It was as if this night had been perfectly designed for the two of us. The air was warm and the breeze was just enough to offer us the fragrances of the daffodils that were blooming alongside the pool. After we had enjoyed our daily five-o'clock martini and were just before opening a bottle of cabernet, the moment of pure bliss happened for me. When Tomas came over and took my head and pressed his forehead against mine, I knew that something spectacular was just about to happen.

The next words that came out of Tomas' mouth were the words, "I really think I would like to marry you". After I expressed with pure glee that the feeling was mutual, we found ourselves in an embrace that seemed to last for hours. The gentle breeze and the floral fragrances seemed to vanish into thin air and all I could feel was the warm touch of Tomas' arms around me and all I could smell was his sweet breath as it caressed my face. It was a happiness that I had never before known. The person that I had fallen deeply in love with had just asked me to spend the rest of my life with him and from the bottom of my gut I screamed, "YES!".

After we let go of each other, we began to discuss when the big event should occur. We both agreed instantly that it should be on our anniversary, July thirty-first would be the day.

It was the typical story: I had always been the pianist, but never the bride. This was to be a different circumstance, however. This time I would be the one walking down the aisle and it had to be perfect. With less than three months to go, there was a lot to be done.

After the date was agreed upon, the next decision was that of a venue that could accommodate a gay wedding in a southern suburb. Tomas and I both wanted a simple and traditional wedding and a small chapel would seem ideal, and it became my mission to arrange for one.

A few short miles from our house stood a tiny chapel that was called Sweetwater Memorial Chapel. It was managed by the Daughters of the American Revolution and I knew that the chances of them allowing a gay wedding there were slim to none (and slim had probably left town) but I was very eager to make that the location for our nuptials.

The lady that answered the phone was very kind when I dialed the number listed for Sweetwater Memorial Chapel. The questions were simple: What is involved in holding a wedding at the Chapel? How much are the usage fees and, how would we get in? The answers were equally as simple: Mail a check in the amount of one hundred-fifty dollars, we'll leave the door open for you. It was that simple. I didn't even have to go into the details of it being a gay wedding. The word wedding must have simply implied the union of one man and one woman. Poetic justice was realized when I was informed that the chapel had begun as a Primitive Baptist Church. Sometime on the date of July thirty-first, some founding members would be rolling in their graves, and two happily married gay men would be dancing.

The location was set and we had a little more than three months to complete the final details of the day. Our next step was to ask the minister to perform the ceremony. Tomas and I had been attending the Metropolitan Community Church of Atlanta up until the time they were asked to leave the building that they had been meeting in every Sunday for the past five years. The congregation had been worshipping at the local Methodist Church until some of the members decided that it wasn't part of their doctrine to allow gays to gather in their facility. The search for our minister began and it wasn't long until we found the lady that had been our spiritual guide for just under a year.

The Reverend Kathy Martin was a dynamic speaker and loving person. My expectations of her reaction were that she would simply say that she would be more than happy to marry Tomas and me. Instead, she informed us that we would need to go through several sessions with her to discuss the importance of marriage and explain to her why we wanted to be married. At first I was insulted at the fact that she didn't just see us as perfect for each other and say that we should definitely be united together in the holy bonds of marriage. Then, I realized that the world was changing, and the marriage of two people of the same sex, who were in love, was beginning to be taken seriously.

The night of our first session arrived and I was filled with anxiety. Tests always terrified me, and this certainly seemed like a test: The most important test of my life, thus far.

The hour long session seemed to go on forever. My fears of having the wrong answers were all that I could think of. How did Tomas seem so cool and collected while I seemed to be a bumbling fool? Whatever it was that came from my lips must have been the right words. Reverend Kathy didn't see the need in seeing us again before the ceremony and she said that we had a sense of love and compassion about us that was undeniable and she would be honored to marry us.

Later that night Connie and Jeanne were going to meet us for a celebratory dinner after we called and told them the good news. During that dinner the question of who should be the entertainment at the reception was asked. As the four of us sat at our table, stumped for ideas, the answer unfurled right before our eyes.

Almost every Sunday night Tomas and I went to Burkhart's, a gay bar downtown, to see a drag show called 'Morticia Deville and the Gospel Echoes'. Morticia was a four- hundred pound drag queen and she was the lead singer on Sunday nights with two very talented back up singers.

As our entourage was completing dinner, Morticia and her boys came in and sat right next to us. It was as if a light went on in all of our heads at the same time. What would be more perfect than a four-hundred pound drag queen singing at the reception of a gay wedding in the back yard of Suburbia, Georgia?! The entertaining threesome agreed.

Everything was falling into place almost effortlessly. Now it was time to get the guest list in order and get the invitations out.

When I called my sister, she was elated and we talked for hours about how much fun it would be and she expressed her joy for me. She asked if I had told our parents yet and I told her that Tomas and I were planning to drive up to their house the following weekend and tell them. She thought that was a better idea than a phone call.

Friday morning arrived and Tomas and I loaded into the Miata, threw the top back, and hit the road for North Carolina. The two of us always managed to have fun in almost any situation. It was going to be a long four and a half hour drive so we stopped at a roadside gas station, grabbed two twenty-four ounce beers, and hopped back in the car. The next thing I new, Tomas had ripped his shorts and shirt off and was waving them in the air. As we were being passed by a truck whose driver was looking down on us, we both laughed at the thoughts of Tomas' naked self in plain view of any car that was taller than a Miata (Which was almost all of them).

We got to my parents house just before dinner and had the usual long-awaited hug session and spent the rest of the evening with idle chat and laughter.

The next morning I joined my mother on the back porch where she sat watching the humming birds and sipping her coffee. Characteristically, I had raised my hopes thinking that my parents would be jubilant with the announcement of my upcoming marriage. That wasn't exactly how reality worked for me that morning.

After I told my mother that Tomas and I were planning our wedding and that I would love nothing more than for them to be there, she informed me that she thought that was why we were there and that she thought it best the we didn't tell my father. It was common knowledge to me that no parent wants their children to go through the trials and tribulations that are presented to a gay person, but I thought that things had progressed further than they had. My father seemed thrilled to sit and talk to Tomas; my mother was always ecstatic with our visits and this seemed like a natural progression to me.

Before Tomas and I left the next day, my mother told us that she loved us both dearly but just didn't understand our relationship and simply couldn't condone it. The words cut like a knife, but Tomas and I both realized that my parents had both been taught that being gay was an abomination in the sight of their God.

The guest list wasn't as I wanted it to be, but as long as the most important person showed up, the one that I was going to dedicate the rest of my life to, I was okay.

July thirty-first came quickly and the morning of the glorious day was to be a hectic one. The lawn had to be cut, the pool needed to be vacuumed, the bar had to be set up, the cake had to be picked up, the food had to be ready to set out immediately after the ceremony, the flowers needed to be placed in the church, everything had to be just perfect for this long awaited day. And at some point Tomas and I had to get ourselves ready to stand in front of God and all of our friends and profess our undying love for one another.

During the midst of the chaos of the day, the phone rang and I answered it. The joy of this day was about to be challenged.

After I hung the phone up, the back door to the house opened and Tomas came out to find me sitting on the back stairs sobbing. "What is wrong?" he questioned. "That was my sister. She isn't coming. Her sister-in-law is going into labor." After I uttered the words, my body began to tremble and I cried harder than before. Tomas took his hand and wiped the tears from my eyes and looked straight into my soul and said, "It's okay. We don't really need anyone else there but us. It's our commitment to each other that matters." His words helped to cheer me and we both got up and attended to the daunting tasks that were before us.

As we stood in the back of the church getting ready for our moment, my thoughts again turned to the founding members of the little chapel that we were standing in. A lot had changed since the 1800's. Instead of the edifice being filled with a bunch of bigots in bonnets, soon it would be filled with a rainbow of cultures: White, black, lesbian, straight, all of them there to witness the union of two men being married by an African American lesbian minister. What an exciting time to be alive.

The first strum of the guitar sounded and the Reverend opened the door and led us to the altar to begin the service. With no best man, no maid of honor, no flower girl or ring bearer, Tomas and I stood alone together at the altar, just the two of us with our Lady of God, and vowed our lives together in the quiet presence of God and in the witness of our true friends.

The service was going beautifully, especially considering the fact that we chose not to have a rehearsal. We had chosen to participate in Holy Communion, however. The bread to be offered was almost a half of a loaf, and Tomas was growing hungry. Our vows were to be recited immediately following the communion and Tomas was to go first. It would be several moments before he could begin to speak, as he had taken more than a mouthful from the loaf of bread and was trying to force it down his throat.

Finally, the vows were stated through tears of joy, the candle symbolizing unity was lit, and two lives became one. Ode to Joy began to fill the air of the chapel and we were all off to celebrate the union of Tomas and Banjo.

The thermometer read 103 degrees and I began to worry about our four-hundred pound drag queen that was hopefully ready, by the pool, to sing us into the night.

By the time Tomas and I reached the house, the party was on. Some of our friends had rushed back to attend to the last minute preparations and everything was just as I had imagined. As the gospel trio began their anthem to welcome us home, I began to look around and realize how blessed I was. Not only had I just married the man of my dreams, but my home and yard were filled with friends from all walks of life.

Morticia and the Echoes wrapped up their portion of the night's entertainment and Tomas and I danced to Elton John's

Something About the Way You Look Tonight. Then there was dancing and laughing for the remainder of the night. It was a night I never wanted to end, but this night ended in a way that will forever touch my heart. The last guest to leave was Justin, and he wished Tomas and me all of the best the world had to offer. ~

Moments of bliss can last in your memories forever. They are the times that are worth holding on to. They are the times that will get you through the tough times that inevitably come along with life. Take pictures of those moments, write them down in a journal, talk about them often. On dark and rainy days, they will bring you light. Bliss will appear at random moments throughout your life and along side it you can EXPECT...

Chapter Twelve
(Surprise)

―⟋⟍―

"To strike with wonder or Amazement"

I t is often said that life is full of surprises. It doesn't matter if you like them or not, in this life you can expect them. Some are good, some are bad, all are necessary to form the life that is yours.

A surprise party in your honor can make you realize that someone cared enough, a surprise phone call can make you realize that someone is gone forever and you should have visited more often. A surprise hug can make a cold winter day seem a little brighter. A surprise knock on the door can make you wish that religious groups would incorporate etiquette into their doctrine, and a surprise look into someone else's world can make you appreciate your own and realize that people are all different, but also the same.

~ It had been six months since the wedding and my life with Tomas couldn't be better. We were constantly surrounded by friends. I still often wondered what my father was doing the day I got married, but what mattered was that we were all still family. Whether or not my father knew that Tomas and I had a wedding, he still treated Tomas as part of the family. My family would come to visit us for long weekends and Tomas and I would travel to be with them every chance we got. It didn't matter anymore that they weren't in our wedding, they were in our lives.

The only people that I had met in Tomas' family so far were his children and ex-wife. Christmas was quickly approaching and we were planning to visit with them in New Hampshire for the holiday.

At this point, it hadn't been revealed to Cassie that Tomas and I were a couple. She assumed I was merely a friend helping Tomas through a difficult time. The rest of his family remained a mystery to me.

When we arrived in New Hampshire I was first surprised at how cold it was. I had never felt a cold that cold in my life. Then, as I looked around I was taken in awe by its beauty. There seemed to be hemlock trees everywhere that were bent over from the weight of the snow as if to bow and welcome us to this winter wonderland. The people were bundled up and rushing around just like they did in all of the Christmas movies I had seen. The snow blew across the open fields in as big of a hurry as the people it landed on. It didn't take me long to learn not to speak. A southern accent seemed to be somewhat of a novelty to the northern folk and I could only imagine that they thought I sounded like a slow learner. Tomas was to do all of the talking from then on. It was, after all, his native tongue.

We had reservations to stay at the finest hotel in the Manchester area. As we drove up to the Bedford Village Inn I was captivated by both its charm and majestic appeal. The hotel was known for its five-star dining, finely appointed rooms and world class service. It was the destination for politicians during the caucuses and election seasons, news anchors that covered such events, and A-list celebrities when they visited the area.

Shortly after we were settled into our room, it was time for Tomas to go and take his kids to dinner and give them their Christmas gifts. I was left alone at the Inn and decided to make myself happy. After exploring the grand inn, I settled into the tavern for a few drinks. Then I wandered back to the room where I intended to make good use of the Jacuzzi. As the tub was filling, I explored the rest of the room. When I opened the night stand drawer and lifted the Gideon Bible, I was completely taken by surprise. Lying right there in the Bedford Village Inn night stand drawer was an un-smoked joint! It didn't seem likely that it was left by the fine Gideon folk, nor by the staff of a fine establishment such as the one I was standing in. My only assumption was that Tomas must have left it for me to relax my nerves while we were in his home land so I took it out, removed my plush robe, and climbed into the tub with it.

Halfway through my mood altering session, the door opened and in walked Tomas. As he inquisitively entered the bathroom, I looked up with a slanted grin and thanked him for his gift. The look of utter dismay on his face was my first clue that he was not the pot toting Santa of the Bedford Village Inn. The next surprise was, again, all mine.

Tomas started laughing and suggested that I put the smoking paper stick out and get dressed. The next phrase is what sent me into a tail spin.

All of Tomas's siblings were in town and staying at a nearby hotel and they had just called him and asked for us to join them for a drink. I threw the joint into a puddle of water and shrieked, "Are you fucking kidding me?! I'm stoned!" He assured me that everything would be okay and that even if his siblings did realize that I was as high as a Georgia pine, they wouldn't care.

As I stumbled out of the tub and into my clothes, paranoia set in. The knowledge of his father not speaking to him anymore set the ball in motion in my dizzied mind. "What if the rest of them are like their father? What if they only told Tomas that his being gay doesn't matter to them but, deep down they really don't approve? And what in the world would they think of my drunk and stoned ass?" My paranoid state of mind was not relieved by Tomas's answer. He only comforted me by saying, "It's okay. Even if they don't know you're stoned, they'll just think you're like this all the time. They will love you."

As we entered the hotel lobby where Tomas' family was staying, I began to pray for an explosion. If not that, the nearest fire alarm. I thought I could easily just pull it and start running. Just as I spotted the nearest pull alarm and exit, we were confronted by one of Tomas' brothers-in-law. Before I could relinquish my thoughts of escaping, I had been introduced and hugged.

The three of us joined the rest of the family in the bar and ordered a couple of beers. Moments after the introductions were made, Tomas decided it would be comical to announce the fact that when he arrived from delivering his children's Christmas gifts, he returned to find me soaking in a tub and smoking a joint. My face turned purple as I held my breath in wait of the response. Boisterous laughter was all I heard. Then one of the sisters said, "You're so lucky. We haven't been able to do that since we had the baby."

The rest of the night was absolutely delightful as Tomas's sisters and brothers began to tell me stories of their childhood and what a trouble maker Tomas had been. They took me in immediately and treated me as if they had known me forever.

The real surprise of the evening came just after the gang all realized Tomas and I had a wedding and they weren't invited. They were appalled! It was so refreshing to be in the middle of this giant family and realize that I was accepted and that they wanted only the best for their brother. It didn't matter who he was married to, as long as he was happy.

After the night ended and just before I fell asleep, I realized a sudden happiness, as once again, I realized what an amazing world ours can be. People that I was terrified of meeting, surprised me with the gift of love. ~

Surprises come in many forms. They are all around us. They're not always welcome, but they come along anyway.

Spontaneous, involuntary surprise is often expressed for only a fraction of a second. It may be followed immediately by the emotions of fear, joy or confusion. The intensity of the surprise is associated with how much the jaw drops, but the mouth may stay closed.

Expect a surprise everyday. Embrace them and let them direct the goodness of your life. With a lot of surprises, EXPECT…

Chapter Thirteen
(Disappointment)

———◊◊◊———

"An event that fails to meet expectations"

Robert Kivosaki described the interaction of disappointment best when he said, "The size of your success is measured by the strength of your desire, the size of your dream, and how you handle disappointment along the way." Thomas Hardy went on to say that "The sudden disappointment of a hope leaves a scar which the ultimate fulfillment of that hope never entirely removes."

The reality of disappointments are unavoidable in life. The bad comes along as well as the good, just not as often. The disappointing times can often overshadow the times when things are good, but there is always a resolve just around the corner. Patience is the tool that we were given to deal with disappointment. With patience and action, disappointments will eventually fade and fall behind the shadows of happiness once again.

~ The neighborhood where Tomas and I lived was a quiet one. It was the typical all-American neighborhood where people worked from nine to five, came home, fed the family, cut the grass, watched television, went to bed and started all over again the next day. It was ironic to me that our lives fit the same mold. Everyone in life seemed to think that gay people were so different and odd just because of who they went to bed with at night. The people in this neighborhood didn't seem to care if we were straight, gay or purple. They liked us and enjoyed our company.

The fact that our lives seemed so similar to the lives of most of the people we knew around us, I began to have a sense of belonging and began to think that the rest of the world may finally be changing and what once was hatred and then tolerance, may finally be becoming acceptance.

When Tomas and I would go back to my hometown to visit with my family, it seemed that the small town had changed along with what I was seeing in my own world. When we all went out for dinner, people would come up to us and seem delighted to see us. Tomas had become a part of my history and people seemed satisfied enough that I had found love and a respectable relationship. Those were the people we saw in restaurants and shops. We hadn't been to church there in a long time and I had forgotten how hatred tasted until we went back to the good old Baptist church again.

It was Mother's Day and I had decided to drive up and surprise my mother by singing a special song for her during the Mother's Day service.

The sanctuary was filled with proud mothers accompanied by their sons and daughters that had joined them for worship on that proud day. My mother was no exception, my sister and I were with her at church and she was beaming with joy.

The time during the service came when I was to take my place behind the pulpit and sing my tribute for my wonderful mother. As I began to leave my seat, I kissed her on the cheek and told her that I loved her. Realizing what I was about to do, she began to smile and cry. That moment brought much joy to me and I proudly marched to my place.

My eyes were on my mother for the entirety of the song and I felt so proud and blessed to be in that very moment. When the last note was released, the congregation applauded me and I returned to sit next to my thankful and radiant mother.

It took only a few seconds for the world to come crumbling down all around me. Instead of hearing a great sermon about the importance of mothers and their relationships with their children, the minister took his stand and began to utter words directed straight towards me. He looked directly at me and began to deliver a speech about how sometimes people need to stop accepting homosexuals and that they need to realize that sometimes *they* even stand up in church and sing the special music.

The next words from the ministers mouth were never allowed to fall upon my ears. As I slammed the door behind me, I began to cry. Anger overtook me as I began to think about how this ignorant man could lead a congregation into judgment and call himself a man of God. He had ruined my mother's special day, and I couldn't find it within myself to forgive him. That was the moment that I vowed never again to darken the doors of the church that raised me and accepted me and promised to love and guide me when I was a child. They had turned their back on me and I was deeply disappointed with the followers of God. I needed to get back to my life, and quickly.

Being suddenly snapped back into a world that was filled with hate began to make me feel depressed and also suspicious of the people around me that expressed their love for me. Did they really mean what they said? Were they only being politically correct by *tolerating* me? Suddenly being tolerated became an insult and I quickly came to despise the term. Tolerance would no longer be acceptable for me. Acceptance was the least that I would tolerate from that moment on.

Life in Atlanta was my saving grace. The people there were too busy to hate me. They all seemed real. If they liked me, they told me; if they didn't like me they told me.

Tomas and I continued our wonderful life in our unique little world and couldn't imagine ourselves being any happier together. We had each other and that really was all that mattered. To find love is to find the greatest treasure on earth. There is no map to lead you to it, only destiny and a willing heart.

A phone call a few months later would prove to be a life changing one for Tomas and me. My mother was on the other end and announced that she was on the way to take my father to the hospital. There was a fifty year difference between my father and me and his health had been declining for several years. It wasn't unusual for me to receive news that he was heading for the hospital again. After a while, you get used to such events. This time seemed different in some way. There was a feeling in my gut that I knew I couldn't push aside.

It wasn't long after I told my boss about the situation that I had gone home, packed a bag and began to head back towards North Carolina.

When I arrived at the hospital I immediately knew that it was all different this time. My father, who was one of the strongest people I had ever known, could barely form a cognitive sentence. He had accepted the fact that for several years he could no longer do everything that he once could, but to see his mind begin to waiver was more than I could handle. The situation had weakened the smile on my mother's face that always welcomed me. It was difficult to see her in such pain and I knew that this time, I would need to be the strong one.

There is a certain sense of denial that develops when it comes to the ones you love. Faith and prayers were expected to simply raise my father out of his situation and bring him home again.

After a couple of days, my sister said that I should take our mom home for the night and let her get some rest and have a nice shower at home. After mom and I had kissed Daddy good-bye for the night, I drove her home and we settled in for a few hours of rest.

Early the next morning, the phone rang and I answered it to hear my sister simply say, "You should get Mom and get here quickly".

Interstate seventy-seven between Elkin and Statesville became a blur as I reached ninety-five miles per hour driving my mother's navy blue Ford Explorer to Davis Hospital. The usual forty-five minute drive was complete within twenty-five minutes as we screeched up to the front of the hospital. When I opened the door to get my mother, Daddy's hair brush fell out and seemingly in slow motion, crashed to the ground. As Mom and I were leaving the house that morning, she ran back in to retrieve it, expecting to brush Daddy's hair when we got to him.

As the automatic doors opened, my mother and I were greeted by my sister and two of my father's friends. The look on their faces announced the dreaded words: Daddy was gone.

Denial was suddenly useless to us and reality washed it away and left us faced with the fact that the man who had loved us and encouraged us for our entire lives, was now in another world and no longer in ours.

My father's wake was very long and a testament to the man who I had always known as Daddy. He had never met a stranger and it was never more obvious than that night. It was almost as if the night of my father's wake was the first time I ever met him. As hundreds of people shook my hand, hugged me and told me how much they loved my father, I realized that this was the legacy I wanted to leave behind when I leave this earth.

Tomas had come to be by my side as soon as I called him and told him the news. Once every few minutes he would come and put his arm around me and ask me if I needed anything during the wake. The looks were those of judgment and disgust, but I realized that the ones who were looking upon me that way, simply didn't know me. I decided to love them anyway. That was what my father had taught me to do.

My father's life had sculpted mine since I was old enough to understand his words and observe his actions. Now, in his death, I began to realize the importance of loving the people around me, whether or not they loved me in return.

The morning of the funeral brought yet another realization. It is true that you should never say never. As we entered the church to say our final farewells to my father, I couldn't help but to be reminded that not many months prior, I had vowed to never step foot into the building that I was now seated in and listening to the praises of my father.

As they lowered my father into the ground, I looked around at all of the people that had come that rainy January morning to say good-bye to this amazing man and was blessed with the thoughts that no box was big enough to hold his life and his spirit. He wasn't in that box, he was all around me.

The morning after the funeral, Tomas and I were leaving to return to our jobs. Saying good-bye to my mother and sister was more difficult than any other time had been. It was going to be a long drive back to Atlanta with all of this sadness in my heart.

Tomas and I had barely gotten out of town when we looked over into the median and saw what was one of the most spectacular things I had ever witnessed before. Flying right next to us at exactly the same speed we were traveling, was a brilliant white dove. It seemed to be looking straight into my eyes as if to comfort me. My father's spirit had come to say good-bye to me and let me know that he was okay, and so was I.

Back in Atlanta, things returned to an awkward normalcy rather quickly. All of our friends began to pour in for evening cocktails, and work resumed every morning just like it always had. The people stuck in traffic with me each morning had no idea of the sadness that was inside of me and they cursed at each other and sped to their busy lives just as they always had.

Summer eventually arrived and Tomas and I opened the pool for the season and I just couldn't imagine life being any other way. Eventually, I got used to calling home and not being able to talk to my father, and my mother and sister were slowly but surely moving on to the next steps in their lives as well. It was as good as it could be. ~

Disenchantment, whether it is a minor disappointment or a major shock, is the signal that things are moving into transition in our lives. Evan Esar once said that hope is tomorrow's veneer over today's disappointment. To hold on to hope is sometimes challenging, especially when the disappointment is the direct shot fired from another human being. To have the hope that people have changed and to realize many remain the same can become a burdensome worry. To face judgment from a fellow man is hurtful. Hope springs eternal and it is up to you to find it and hold on to it. The impressions that other people have of you can only change if you show them who you truly are. Be patient with them; lay fear and hatred aside and use the abilities that you have to change someone's mind. Ignorance can't be fought with ignorance but the seeds of love will bloom. When people disappoint you, consider it a lesson that is for you to learn.

The patience that it takes to overcome disappointment can be frustrating. Sometimes it will be followed with a lot of work on your part and with it you can EXPECT...

Chapter Fourteen
"Sacrifice"

—◦◦◦—

(The surrendering of something important
for the sake of something else)

One of the most difficult things in life is to sacrifice something you love for someone you love. It is the true test of a relationship. It is the true test of your character and it most often involves the shedding of tears and a feeling of significant loss. There are times in life when it is necessary to sacrifice something for other people around you. It is the time when you will grow as a person. After the initial loss of what you once thought to be the most important thing in the world, a sense of dignity and rightness ensues. To grow through sacrifice involves a great deal of giving, patience, and trust. It is rare that sacrifice will not be rewarded. Look ahead and not behind. To get, you must first give.

~ Life for Tomas and myself continued to be a sort of gay couple in the suburbs fairytale. Our neighbors would invite us over for cookouts, our friends were always stopping in for drinks around the pool, and we continued to go dancing almost every weekend.

One afternoon as I returned home from work, I was met at the top of the stairs by Tomas. He had already had one martini and was now working on another one. When I asked him what was going on, he announced that he had been laid off from work. He had been a chemist for Coca-Cola for several years and suddenly fell victim to the Affirmative Action movement. He was devastated. He had a work ethic that was unparalleled and he was loyal to a fault.

The company had given Tomas a considerable severance package which allowed him several months to figure out what his next step would be. After several phone interviews, a candle company flew him to New Hampshire for an interview and shortly thereafter, asked him to join their company.

Tomas was very excited about the new position as it would place him minutes away from his children. The news wasn't very welcome to me. It meant that I would be a distance away from what I had left in my family that would not be considered drivable. My mother's heart would surely be broken by this news. It was news that I was terrified of delivering to my mother who was still lonely and grieving the loss of my father.

One brief phone call to my sister solved the problem. She offered to tell the breaking story to mom for me.

Just as I had anticipated, the next step in my life came as a shock to my mother and it was a tearful face that proved it.

She explained to me that she understood the situation but was devastated that I would be so far away.

The time came quickly and we had a lot to do. Tomas moved up to New Hampshire, rented a two room apartment, and began his new chapter.

Prior to all of these events, I had interviewed with Delta Airlines for a position as a flight attendant. It had been a while since I had heard anything from them regarding the position and two days after Tomas left, I received notice that they wanted to offer me the job. A brief conversation with the hiring office for Delta left me with a sinking feeling. The dream of flying for a living was short lived. The position was only available in Atlanta and they had no need for a flight attendant in Manchester, New Hampshire. Tomas had been knocked down pretty hard by losing his job and was now very excited about his new one. I didn't have the heart to tell him that I had been disappointed as well.

Our house was finally sold and my mom and sister came to help me pack everything up for the movers to haul away. The three of us worked very hard and we decided that since it may be a while before we could see each other again, that we might as well play hard too. A lot of margaritas were consumed by the pool in the evenings and we sat and talked for hours… usually until the sun came up.

The dreaded morning approached and I kissed my mom and sister good-bye and watched them head up the street back towards their settled lives. The little Miata was packed and it was time for me to say good-bye to what I had known as a wonderful life up until now.

There was one final thing that had to be done before I left for my long and tiring drive to New England: I had to say good-bye to Connie and Jeanne. To say good-bye to friends that you have been with almost every night for years and head off to a brand new world where you know nobody but your significant other is a painful and frightening thing to do.

Tears were shed and long hugs were given and received and I backed out of Connie and Jeanne's driveway with so many tears in my eyes that I could barely see to where I was backing up. But it was time to go and I wiped my tears and put the car in drive and headed to my new and unknown existence.

Fear was once again in the forefront of my mind as Tomas had informed me that New Hampshire was not a gay friendly place and I was concerned about how I would be received there. There had been a human rights campaign fund sticker on my car for years. It never led to any trouble in Atlanta, but fearing the unknown, I didn't have the balls to announce right off the bat to my new peers that I was gay, so I peeled the bill board off of my bumper before I entered the great north.

As I pulled around the corner onto Orange Street in Manchester, my jaw dropped when I realized where our new accommodations were. The apartment that Tomas had given me directions to was on a busy and crowded street directly across from a Catholic church. As I stopped the Miata and got out, I was shocked to see my breath in the middle of the afternoon in July. This, Dorothy, was not in Kansas anymore.

I approached the building that was going to be what I called home for an unspecified amount of time and began to search for the key that Tomas had placed for me on the front porch.

After I located the key, I knew I was at the right place so I cautiously approached the back door. Quietly placing my face to the window, I smelled candles and knew that this must be the door to the new kingdom, so I turned the key, opened the door, and began my exploration of the mysterious looking building.

The first thing I saw as I entered the apartment was a blow-up mattress on the brown indoor-outdoor carpet. It was in a small room that wasn't much larger than the mattress itself. Right next to this tiny room was a galley kitchen that was so small I wondered if they had to build the building around the refrigerator. That was the only way I could imagine they got one in there.

When the disbelief of the tiny apartment began to subside, I saw an open door and wandered through it. The room on the other side was a little larger and hosted a great window that overlooked one of the city streets that surrounded the building. There was another door, which thrilled me. I just knew that this couldn't be all there was to where Tomas and I would be living. After opening the door, I was instantly snapped back to the reality of my small world. Beyond that door was a great hallway that led to the front entrance of the building and to other apartments. I had often heard of two room apartments but never realized that they truly were two rooms. This was going to be a challenge.

After settling into my reality, the search began for the most important contents of the two small rooms. I needed to find the gin bottle and I needed to find it quickly. It couldn't be too difficult of a search, there were only four cupboards to look in.

The gin and vermouth were there and two martini glasses were located in the freezer. The day was just starting to brighten up for me. The rest of the afternoon was spent on the porch with a sweatshirt over my tank-top and a martini in my hand, watching my breath as it hit the cool air of July as I sat and waited for my beloved husband to get home from work. ˜

The good in life most often is the result of sacrifice in some form or another. Lives were sacrificed and lost for your freedom, pain was the sacrifice for the birth of your precious life, forgiveness is the sacrifice for your survival from bullies and people who can't accept you for who you are. Sacrifice is the gateway to ultimate reward. In order for a tulip to bloom in the Spring, it must endure the reality of a brutal Winter.

Once the ingredients of sacrifice have all been blended and the recipe is complete, the blessings will follow. After the initial sacrifice is over, it is most likely that you can EXPECT...

Chapter Fifteen
"To Settle"

—⟨∿⟩—

(Come to rest. To become fixed, resolved or established)

After years of wandering and searching for a place to belong, the sense of finally feeling settled is a comfort that is like no other. To be settled with someone you love can make any place, whether strange or familiar, feel like home. Sometimes you have to settle for a place that frightens you at first, but once you settle there with someone who loves you, it will become the magnet of your heart.

—⟨∿⟩—

~ Three months had gone by since Tomas and I had been residents of New Hampshire. The search for a new home had been a tiresome effort, but with patience and long days looking, we finally found a house that we believed would be perfect for the two of us.

The previous owner had completely renovated the inside and it was done with high-end appointments and there wasn't much for Tomas and I to do but to move in. The two extra bedrooms would be perfect for Tomas' kids to come over and stay with us every other weekend as it was decided by Tomas and Cassie and incorporated into their divorce decree.

The job at the candle company was going well for Tomas and it was time for me to begin a search for employment as well. It was through a temp agency that I was placed in a position in a computer sales company answering the phones and filing various forms. Without much interaction from the other employees there, I went in every day and performed my given tasks to the best of my ability. Before long I was approached by the owner of the company's wife and was asked if I would be interested in a permanent position with the company in the sales department. I was honored that my work ethic and skills had been noticed by someone so high up on the totem pole as she was and I gratefully accepted her offer.

It wasn't long after I had been moved upstairs to the good ole boys club that things began to be awkward. It was the females that I befriended as I had no idea how to converse with the guys about what ever sport had been on television the night before. After joining the girls in a holiday cookie swap, the looks and snarls from the guys became more and more obvious and before long, early in the morning as I was dressing for work, I received a phone call from one of the managers stating that my services were no longer necessary. With it being common knowledge that New Hampshire is an at-will employment state, I realized I had no legal right to argue the cause of my dismissal, so I simply replied with a polite thank-you and asked that they keep me in mind if anything else came up that would be suitable for me.

Since there wasn't a blow job department, I knew that it wasn't likely that I would be hearing anything else from them.

After a few weeks, I found an ad in the paper for a position as a flower processor at a local floral wholesaler. After my first interview, I was offered the job and, rather quickly, I began to realize just how different Yankees are from Southerners as I was informed that my duties began at six o'clock in the morning.

After a few days at my new job, I became used to the hours and enjoyed having the leisure of having a good deal of the afternoons off. People in the floral industry, whether straight or gay, seemed much different than any others that I had met in the great north thus far. My sexuality didn't bother them, and theirs didn't bother me.

As time went on, I began to develop friendships that would be long lasting. There was one guy at work that seemed kinder than all of the rest and I would spend my spare time at his desk talking to him. He told me stories of his wife and how his life was, and eventually I realized that it was time for me to unleash my big gay secret. The words were received graciously by my new friend, Ben, and his reply was simple: "We all assumed it, but we figured you would tell us on your own terms". It was as if I had been welcomed home for the first time in a very long time. Ben and I began doing things together after work. We would go bike riding and kayaking almost every other day and would end up back at my house to have martinis and wait for Tomas to return home from work. It took a while for Tomas to warm up to the idea of Ben and I hanging out together as he assumed that no straight man would hang out with a gay guy as much as he did with out expecting something in return.

Eventually Tomas and Ben became as good of friends as Ben and I were and the three of us would stand in our kitchen several times a week and have drinks. It was a refreshing change to have a straight person around that wasn't afraid of his own sexuality and could just hang out and laugh with us. The reassurance that the world didn't hate me was a very welcome addition to our new home.

Before long, there was hardly a night that went by that we didn't have a friend over for dinner and drinks. It was becoming like the old days back in Atlanta and our home was filled with music and laughter once again.

The neighborhood we lived in still remained a mystery as to how we were being received there. The night that our furniture had arrived was our first indication as to what most of our new neighbors thought about the gays moving in. Our female realtor had stopped by to see how everything was going and Tomas was in the driveway chatting away with her while I was inside directing the movers as to what box went into which room. During this process a married couple from down the street stopped by to welcome their new neighbors with a plate full of home made cookies and were busy assuming that Tomas and our real estate agent were the nice couple moving in.

After several minutes of idle chit-chat in the driveway, I walked outside in search of a missing box. Simultaneously, one of the movers was asking Tomas where something belonged. Tomas looked at me and asked me where the item in question was to be positioned. After I told the mover where to put the arm full of items, I walked over and was introduced to the lovely parents of five. Suddenly there was a look of terror on the gentleman's face as he slowly put two and two together. Seconds later, the obviously offended couple was trotting away from the house of queens as quickly as their straight-laced sneakers would carry them.

Our questions were answered in that very moment and we realized that we should probably spend most of our time either in the house or in the back yard.

It wasn't long afterwards that the older lady directly across the street from us was placed into an assisted living residence and we were getting new neighbors. Tomas and I watched closely as they moved in. Finally, we decided it was time to meet them and we walked across the street to welcome them and offer introductions.

We were warmly received and offered cold drinks. Tomas and I were pleasantly surprised that they didn't seem to mind the fact that we were obviously not brothers. Not only did they figure out our situation, but they didn't care one way or another. We were later informed that we were the only people in the neighborhood that took the time to welcome them and how much they appreciated the fact that we did. They told us we seemed like very good people and that we should get together for dinner sometime. That is what we did a few times a week from that night on.

As our new neighbors began to meet some of our other neighbors, the topic of the two boys across the street was often brought up. Eventually, after our new friends began to speak of the great times we all had together to our other neighbors, the social climate began to change. One evening, just before dusk, Tomas and I were across the street for a visit and one of the other neighbors rang the door bell. The gentleman was asked in and offered a drink. As the night progressed, the conversation turned to the subject of homosexuality. The strange thing was, the subject wasn't thrown out by Tomas or myself, it was the new guy that began discussing the lifestyle that Tomas and I led. Much to our dismay, he wasn't there to judge us. He was there to let us know that before our arrival in his neighborhood, he had preconceived notions about gay people. He went on to say that since Tomas and I had been living there, his views had changed drastically. Now, instead of only being exposed to the gay culture by his television when the news would only broadcast the extreme gays during gay pride season, he saw two wonderful human beings that were the kindest people who had lived in our house, and were willing to do things for neighbors that, up until now, nobody else had.

This man's apologetic speech touched Tomas and I to the point of tears. Realizing that we had changed a families views about what they assumed we were was a monumental moment. The realization that we could change the world by simply being kind to people who weren't comfortable with us was rapturously enlightening.

Soon after that night Tomas and I were sitting around having dinner and I told him that I wanted to have a party and invite the entire neighborhood. The holidays were coming and it would be the perfect time for an open house. At that point, not many homes had been opened up to us by others in the neighborhood, so we decided we would open ours up to them.

Our home was decorated to the nines on that cold December evening as Tomas and I stood in the kitchen waiting to see who, if anyone, would accept our invitation. The hours listed were from seven o'clock in the evening until nine o'clock. It was now seven-fifteen and it was still only the two of us. As I began to be questioned as to why I had purchased so much wine and bought so much food and labored over it all day, my head began to sink and just before a tear could make it out of my tear ducts, the door bell rang.

When Tomas and I first reached the front door, we saw a couple that we had never seen before holding a bottle of wine to offer their hosts. We opened the door and were introduced to the couple and before we could take their coats for them, there was a procession of neighbors walking towards our home. After a half-hour receiving line, the house was full of holiday music and all of the neighbors getting reacquainted, and the air was filled with laughter. The entire neighborhood showed up. Tomas and I were amazed as each and every one of them thanked us and told us how important of an event that it was as nobody in the neighborhood had ever done anything like that before. They were thrilled and very grateful. And suddenly, it was Christmas on Random Road in Bedford, New Hampshire.

The most unexpected guest arrived around eight-fifteen. The bell rang and I meandered my way through the forty-some odd people that were in different conversational groups and answered the door. The oldest lady in the neighborhood was standing in the doorway when I got there and before I could utter a single word, I was greeted with these words: "Hi, I'm Betsy Goddard, where's the bar?". I knew immediately that I would enjoy this guest most of all.

The last guest left at eleven-fifteen and Tomas and I stood in amazement at how well the evening had gone. It had been a success and people were starting to warm up to us. We were no longer the house that people would suddenly burst into a sprint to avoid, but now we were the house where people would stop just to say hi and ask how our lives were going. We had made a difference and it felt wonderful.

It became thrillingly realized that Tomas and I hadn't simply settled for a house in a random neighborhood, but we had settled into a home in a warm and loving neighborhood. We simply had to reach out for the acceptance and respect that we had long desired. ~

There is a great difference in simply settling and settling. If you allow yourself to simply settle for the environment that surrounds you, you are robbing yourself from the great blessing of life. To actually reach into your own life and discover it, and to let your love slowly seep into the lives of others, you can eventually settle into a life of abundant rewards. One of the greatest challenges to overcome is to learn the difference between settling for and settling into. When you settle into a life and begin to earn the respect of those around you, it is time to EXPECT...

(Interlude)

~ The year 2000 was a difficult one for my family but it was especially difficult for my sister. Not only had we lost our father, but her husband had left her and after I moved to New Hampshire, she felt that I had left her as well.

Her life began to change for the better after a while as she found a man that truly loved her and they eventually became inseparable. Not long after that, they became engaged.

It was during my annual Christmas trip back to North Carolina that the happy couple told me about their big plans. My sister asked me not only if I would decorate the church and reception hall for the event, but also asked me if I would be her maid-of- honor. I was delighted!

The wedding was in April and it was to take place in a small town that the two had fallen in love with and spent their weekends there.

A few weeks after I returned to New Hampshire I received one of the most difficult phone calls I had ever received. My sister had breast cancer.

April was coming quickly and my sister was determined to go on with the plans to marry her Mr. Wonderful on the day that they had planned…no matter what.

Love Valley is a place like no other I've ever seen. The streets are all dirt and most of them are closed off to vehicular traffic because the mode of transportation of choice is horses. There is a tiny chapel on top of a hill that overlooks the valley and that chapel was now days away from being filled to capacity with the wonderful people my sister and her soon to be husband had to surround them with love and support.

The day when I arrived was going to be a very busy one as I had previously shipped many boxes that were full of silk flowers, silk ribbon, toulle, florist's wire, hot glue sticks and shear fabric which was intended to drape the chapel and the reception hall.

The place where we were staying was situated right in the middle of this strange little town and right next to the tack shop. (A tack shop is the equivalent of the local mechanic, as that is the place the cowboys all take their horses to be repaired.) There was a long front porch on the cottage and since it was such a beautiful day, I decided to perch myself there with my box of trinkets and begin tying the fifty some odd bows that I needed to make my sisters vision come to life.

When I first took my seat on the front porch, everything seemed to be going normally. The cowboys next door didn't seem to mind that I was there, the people on horses continued on their journeys down the dirt roads as if I were nowhere to be seen.

Things began to take on a different look as I pulled the first of the cream colored silk ribbon out of the box and began forming them into perfect bows. The sounds that were coming from the tack shop moments ago suddenly stopped. The sound of hooves striking the earth stopped. The entire town seemed to fall silent. When I looked up to see what had happened, I realized that I was what happened. It hit me that I was probably the only real life gay person that these people had ever seen. I was the big pink elephant. With my hands beginning to tremble with fear, I continued my task, uninterrupted by sound or inquiry.

After completing my job of decorating the town for a wedding, it was now time to get ready for the ceremony and make sure that I had attended to all of the duties that I knew a maid-of-honor was responsible for.

Several weeks prior to my arrival at Love Valley, my sister had bestowed yet another honor upon me. In the absence of our father, nothing would please her more than to have me walk her down the aisle and give her away to the man that she would be spending the rest of her life with.

The moment finally arrived and it was time to enter the church with this beautiful bride that was my sister and my best friend.

She had never looked more beautiful than she did at that very moment and her smile had never been brighter as she looked down the aisle and saw the man she was completely in love with standing there with a matching smile and waiting for me to place my sisters hand into his.

After the walk was over, I took my place next to my sister and she handed me her bouquet. That was the first time I looked out into the congregation. Some of the looks on some of the peoples faces were that of confusion and disbelief. "Don't the guys belong on the other side?" was what I'm sure most of them were thinking. As I put a huge and gleaming smile on my face, I looked around at how beautiful the chapel looked and then turned to watch my sister and stood as her maid-of-honor as one of the happiest and proudest gays on earth at that very moment. ~

Chapter Sixteen

"Acceptance"

━━━◦◦◦━━━

(The quality or state of being accepted or acceptable)

To reach the point of acceptance by those around you can sometimes be a battle. It is a battle worth fighting. Often times people simply don't accept you because they are ignorant to the person that lies within you. What people see on the outside is most often how they judge you. It is up to you to let them see what is on the inside. It is a book that only you can open…and the world needs to read it.

━━◦◦◦━━

~ It has been eleven years since our first holiday neighborhood soiree and the neighbors are all still excited to stop by and see the boys. Some of them have become like family to us. We join them for dinner, they stop by for drinks, we have been invited to the weddings of their children, and we've been to the funerals of some of the older neighbors. It all happened because we reached out to others instead of waiting for them to reach out to us. Our love for other people spread throughout a community and it continues to grow.

The friendships that I have with my mother and sister continue to grow as well. At least a couple of times a week my mother and I will talk on the phone for several hours. One very cold night in January we were talking and it was nearly one o'clock in the morning. That time of the year the conversation is usually more of a monologue than it is dialogue as I'm usually bitching about the weather. This night was different. The subject of young people being bullied to the point of taking their own lives is what we were discussing. It was a subject that had reduced me to tears many times over the previous months. The statement I made to my mother led to one of the most memorable conversations my mother and I have ever had in the forty-two years since she gave birth to me. "I don't know how I ever made it through this" was what I said to her. Her reply delivered the warmest feeling of love that a child could receive from his mother. "I don't know either, son. I wish I would have know better how to handle things back then, but I just didn't." She then went on to say, "When I think about you, son, I feel so blessed. Sometimes I feel like the Virgin Mary, as I have given birth to one of the most wonderful and unique people on the earth." The words stopped me dead in my tracks and I began to cry. At that very moment I knew that something had to be done about all of the kids who may not have the strength to make it through by themselves. I had to find a way to let them know that life won't always be easy, but it won't always be as tough, either. I had to let you know what to EXPECT!

Chapter Seventeen
"EXPECT!"

———⌇———

When I was just a small child I knew that something was different about me from the rest of the boys I hung out with. It was my belief that there were many more people like me in society and that I was part of a special club. With the innocent knowledge that I was born into the body that God trusted me with, I believed that the world kept people like me in the darkness about who I was and that when I turned a certain age it would be revealed to me that I was part of a special group and that I hadn't been told what my situation was because I was so special. Assuming there were many more like me, I believed that at a predetermined point in my life I would be celebrated and welcomed into the club. (I also believed that all cats were girls and all dogs were boys!)

As I got older the reality became clear. There was no special club and there would be no coming out party like the ones for debutantes. I was on my own with this and I thought it had to be kept secret because during the years I was dealing with it, I was told that people like me were sick and certainly damned to hell. But I was, without a doubt, special. My heart was different from those of a lot of people that I had known. I had been taught to love others more than myself and I had a heart that was more compassionate towards others than most. I was the only person I knew that cried when overweight people dropped their food before they got it home. Somehow that was entertaining to some people. It worried me. Strangers always intrigued me. To make friends out of them was my greatest mission.

The word gay is defined as happily excited, merry; keenly alive and exuberant. That is what I was and still am. The joy that lives in my heart cannot be defeated by the hatred or ignorance of another human being; I can only do that myself. You have that in you as well.

After wondering for several years why some people were so mean to me, it became clear to me. People can sense when you are hiding something. If you have an insecurity, some people will try to keep their own insecurities in the dark by trying to bring yours into the light. Whether or not is consciously done or subconsciously, some people will try to put negative focus on you to keep others from seeing what their deep fears are. Bullies are simply hiding from a deep-rooted issue; they have troubles of their own.

When the person that bullied me the most in high school came up to me years after graduation and apologized, it shocked me. Instead of continuing to hold a grudge, I simply told him that I understood and that I forgave him. When he inquired as to how I could be so forgiving, I simply told him that I was raised to love and not hate and then I told him I knew he was just hiding the fact that he had the smallest penis in the entire school. And we laughed together.

Bullying comes in many forms. Sometimes your biggest bully is your own fear.. Don't be afraid of who you are. Own who you are and be comfortable in your own skin. If you're not, other people can't be comfortable in your presence, either.

What ever point you are at within your own life, be honest. If you are just a young child and realize that you're not into the same things that your friends are, find someone to talk to. Look for someone that will understand you. You are far too important to go through those struggles alone. There are a lot of options for you. People, like me, that have been through what you are going through are here for you. We have great stories and we'd love to share them with you. We've been there; we know it sucks. We also know that life gets so much better. Life won't always be a bowl of cherries, but it won't always be a sack of crap, either.

Expect challenges all throughout life. Don't feel unique because life throws you a curveball. Life does that to everybody. Your challenge is different.

Being part of a minority can be tough enough. Having a different skin color than someone else can create a difficult situation and people who are visibly different from others can't hide from that. It is a sad and dangerous truth that you can actually hide from your uniqueness. Please don't. Not only will you eventually end up hurting yourself, you will also hurt many people around you.

There are a lot of people out there that marry people of the opposite sex because they are afraid of how the truth of being gay will effect their own life. Don't be that selfish. You are hurting someone else to cover your own ass. That is wrong. Be strong and have the courage to be the great person you were intended to be. You can never reach your full potential

153

as a person if you are hiding your true self behind a wall of deceit.

There have been several people throughout my life that were hiding behind the safety of marriage. The ones who eventually came to terms with their situation and were honest to their spouses about it were the ones that came out ahead of the game. The ones who remained in their bed of lies until they eventually were caught up with suffered the most. There have been several people that I have met along my own journey who were in that boat. The truth didn't kill them, it set them free. It also gave freedom and true joy to the ones that they had been lying to all along. Most truths like that have a sting when first aired, but given time, all wounds heal.

No matter what your situation is, someone else has been, or is, going through it as well. You're never alone. Some celebrities and famous athletes are going through the same struggles as you are. It is my greatest desire that some day we will live in a world where they can be themselves as well. Hopefully it will be while they are young and can show the world that being gay is not what defines them, but their talents are what makes them shine. Maybe someday they will realize that they can make a huge difference in the world and perhaps save a life by being the type of role model that can show others that we're all okay.

People from all walks of life are on the same battlefield that you are fighting on. Politicians, ministers, school teachers, even the quarter back at your school. We come from different backgrounds and social environments. One thing unites us: the desire to be accepted and loved for who we are. As the old song says, We are Family…one great big human family.

Chapter Eighteen
"Do the Right Thing"

—⊰ဗ/ဗ⊱—

One afternoon while I was enrolled in the Church of God college that I attended in Tennessee, there was a knock on my door and the campus pastor's assistant was on the other side. He informed me that the pastor wished to speak to me in his office at once. When I arrived at the pastor's office, I was taken by surprise to find that he had also summoned Parker to the same meeting. Someone had been to the pastor and told him that Parker and I had been involved in homosexual activities. We were there to be chastised.

There was a park in Chattanooga that a friend had told me about. It was where gay men went to find other gay men. After going there several times, I had become comfortable with the environment and would often go there and hang out with other guys like me. One sunny afternoon, a few of us were sitting by the river talking and I looked up to see the campus pastor, whose office I was now sitting in, cruising the park and talking to other men as well. After seeing the look of shock and fear on my face, one of my friends asked me what was wrong. As soon as I informed him of the situation, my friend burst into hysterical laughter and began to tell me that he sees that dude here all the time and that he even knew a guy that had serviced him in his car.

After several minutes of this hypocritical man of God chastising Parker and myself, telling us that we were sick and would go straight to hell if we didn't turn to God for deliverance, I couldn't take it anymore. "How can you sit behind that desk and sling a Bible at us?" was my question. With a perplexed look on his face, the pastor asked me what I was talking about. At that moment I was faced with a very important choice. I could either scream and rant because he was judging me for his own actions, or I could offer him support and sympathy for the situation that he had placed himself in. To be the bigger person is not always the easiest thing in life to do, but it is always the right thing to do. After I informed the pastor that I was aware of his extra curricular activities in the park, I also told him that I wouldn't judge him for it and assured him that his secret was safe with me. Nothing good could have come from me outing the pastor. He had made the decisions to lie to his wife and family and to his congregation. It was up to him to lie in the bed that he had made for himself or get out of it and clean the sheets.

Shortly after the pastor informed Parker and me that he was only in the park to minister to the sinners that frequented the place, we were invited to leave his office.

I was never invited back to the pastor's office again and that was fine with me. The feeling of doing the right thing was all I needed to take from that scenario. My life would continue and I could live in the freedom that is honesty. He would continue to be stuck in his personal hell. Years later, I can now look back at that situation and hold my head up high. His judgments didn't matter to me then, and they don't matter to me now.

Every situation in life is temporary. The world continues to go on living life and that's what we must do. After you make it through a trial, and if you do the right thing, you will look back at it one day and be thankful for the lesson you learned from it. Eventually, what originally happened won't matter at all. Life has a way of moving you forward.

Chapter Nineteen
"Do Unto Others"

O ne of the most important things that will get you to a place of happiness is to remember the most important rule of life: The golden rule. It is my greatest belief that putting others needs before my own and giving of myself joyously is what has made my life so fulfilling. When you are kind to others, it is almost impossible for them not to give love back to you in return.

It has been years since I have seen many of the people from my past. Thanks to social networks on the internet, I have been able to reconnect with many of them. Often times throughout life I have wondered what people have thought about me and if I have lived a decent life that showed the world that I loved it. Many blessings have been bestowed up on me by having contact now with people from my past. Very often I hear from an old friend that tells me how much they miss me and what a difference I have made in their lives. There isn't much more in the world that is more rewarding than to hear those words.

The best time to start living a rewarding life is right now. Sometimes you will need to apologize to people. Sometimes you will need to hear an apology from someone else. Always forgive. Know that forgiveness is actually for you and not the person that you are forgiving. It is a heavy burden to carry a grudge. Let it go and you will find a comfort like no other. Forgiving is freeing.

If you need to be forgiven, don't be afraid to swallow your pride and ask for it. That, too, is freeing. It has been very surprising to me how willing people are to forgive. All they need in order to offer you forgiveness is permission from you.

This past Christmas was an inspirational one for me. Going back to my home town for Christmas has been the highlight of my year since Tomas and I moved to New Hampshire. This year was one of the best yet. Over the internet I posted that I would be at a certain restaurant on the day I arrived back home. I posted an invitation on my wall and before I knew it, there were thirty people that wanted to get together with me and celebrate old times with old friends.

As I sat around the bar during that evening, my life began to unfold around me. Blessings were abundant as I looked around in awe at the people from my life and realized what a wonderful and varied group they all were. Some were my age, some older and some younger. Male and female, gay and straight. I realized then that I had accomplished one of my lifetime goals: To touch the lives of people from all walks of life and have them all come together in unison and celebrate life itself.

To come to a place of great joy and happiness, you must offer a smile and an open heart and mind. The rest will fall in place. People migrate towards a happy person. That is what you can be. The greatest advice my father ever gave to me was, "To have friends, you must show yourself friendly". To have true friends, you have to be comfortable with who you are. Own who you are, be comfortable in your own skin. Otherwise, people won't be able to be comfortable around you.

Chapter Twenty
"Be Different...Be You"

Realizing that you are different from everyone around you can be a horrifying discovery. Realizing that you can actually embrace that difference and live a happy and fulfilling life can be the most spectacular realization of your life.

When I first began to experience the fear that others had of me because I was different, I was horrified. I also knew that there was nothing I could do about it. When I first decided to express myself by dressing differently than everyone else, it was almost magical. Some people still laughed and taunted me, but my decision forced me into a place where there were other people like me. Before I fashionably announced myself to the world, I was simply a gay kid that was open to ridicule. Trying to fit in just wasn't going to work for me and I had to realize it, accept it and move on. Before I knew it, other kids were actually imitating my sense of style. Football players were even borrowing my hair cut.

The group of friends that chose me was a very happy group. We were always in the hallways at school laughing together and helping each other through whatever drama had forced itself into our lives.

Happiness attracts happiness and misery and hatred attract misery and hatred. You have a choice. Your smile can be your guide. Let it shine and the world will put its arms around you eventually. Nothing happens over night, especially a friendship.

A smile is how every friendship in New Hampshire has begun for me. Some very special people have entered my life in this place that I was so frightened to be in. No matter where you are in life, smile. Someone out there is looking for it… someone like you.

Chapter Twenty-One
"Beat the Bully"

Your own fears and doubts are your biggest bullies. Don't be afraid to face them. Be excited to let go of them.

Life is a journey that is comprised of many roads. Some are paved and easy to travel, some are dirty and bumpy and not easily passed. There are bridges along the way that you must cross in order to reach your place of well-being. Don't hesitate to cross them. What lies behind when you cross the bridge was only there to bring you to the next path. Cross the bridge and don't look down. The waters below may seem inviting but don't jump into them. Keep going, the other side of the bridge is welcoming you and wants to embrace you. The waters below are dark and lonely but the path ahead of you is strewn with warmth and friendliness. But you must cross the bridge in order to experience its freedoms.

There were many times in my life when I thought that I simply couldn't take what was happening to me. To end my life was sometimes very tempting. When I felt like an absolute freak and complete misfit, a bottle of pills and a warm tub to drown in seemed to be the only answer.

Being told that I was sick and bound for a fiery hell, suicide often beckoned me. There were many nights that I would lie in my dorm room in college and consider how would be the best way to end my life. Feelings of inadequacy flooded my every thought. Knowing that I couldn't change the way I felt and believing that those feelings were the most horrible feelings to have, I couldn't imagine my life getting any better.

Finding people like me that I could confide in was my only salvation. With all of the resources you have today, you have the greatest of opportunities to overcome what ever your bully is. Reach out. There are many people that want to help you and love you. You are a gift to us from God. Don't take that away from us.

Hopefully some day you will look back at *Expect* and realize that someone was spared just to tell you the story. You will have a story to tell some day as well, and there will be someone who needs to hear it.

After the light finally shined on my soul, I realized that, not only could I change myself, but I could change the way others viewed me. I didn't quit. I didn't give up. I kept going and my life got better and better…and it continues to. You have that power as well. The dark times of my life were necessary. They were tests to prove my true grit. Be thankful for them. They are only preparing you to move on into a place of fulfillment and belonging. There is a place for you. Don't be a coward and give up. Keep searching and you will find it. Or if you're truly lucky, it will find you.

The greatest thing I've learned is that you can never know exactly what to expect in life. Once you realize that not knowing what to expect can be one of the best parts of life, you will finally start to live.

It is also important to realize that not everyone will like you. While it's a true blessing to know who your friends are, it's equally important to know who is not your friend. Look at Oprah, not everybody likes her, but she did pretty damn good in spite of it.

Live your life to your fullest potential. It may not be what others expect from you but don't ever give up, don't ever settle, don't be afraid but always EXPECT!

~ Postlude ~

~~ As I sit and write my final words to you, I want you to know that you are loved. It is my greatest desire for you to become the amazing person that is hiding within your soul. Let that person out. Some people won't accept it at first and that's okay. They don't own your world, you do. Never fight fire with fire. Everyone gets burned that way. Fight it with cooling waters of love. Ignorance is not bliss, it is to be pitied. Remember that people that try to hurt you are only hiding from their own pains and suffering.

Always aim for the head of the nail when building the house that is your life. Of course you'll miss once in a while and hit your thumb. Go ahead and jump around and swear a while, the pain will subside. There's no sense cutting your thumb off because it hurts. It's the same scenario with your life. Sometimes you will hurt. You don't need to end your life because of pain. It will pass. Take it from someone who has been there.

Because I never gave up; because I never quit, my life has been a life that I would envy if it wasn't mine. I've been able to

STEVE
BULBIRD
Marcin
FRIEND

travel the world with my amazing husband that I was blessed to finally find. Friendships abundantly surround me every day. A family full of love and support is always by my side. Don't let the bad things in life be the melody of your life. Listen for the harmony that is the underlying happiness of your soul.

After fourteen years, Tomas and I still have a martini together every single night and discuss our day with each other. As I finish telling you my story, Tomas is in the kitchen of the lake house that we built together, shaking a martini, and waiting to hear how my story ends.

Once you look beyond today and into the brightness of tomorrow, a life of joy, numerous friendships, love and acceptance is what you can EXPECT.

** The choices I made throughout my life weren't always the right ones; they weren't all wrong, either. After reading *Expect* you may think I could have handled some things differently. That's the thing about life. Had I not done some of the things that I've done, I wouldn't be where I am today. I wouldn't have found happiness. You may also think I drink too much. My mother would agree with you. As I've said before, *Expect* isn't a guideline for a life for you, it's just to let you know that I care about you and I want you to find the happiness in life that I have. I love you.

If you feel that you have nobody else to talk to regarding your situation, please feel free to contact me. I promise that I want to hear from you. I will listen and help you anyway that I can. banjomartini@yahoo.com wants to hear from you.

CPSIA information can be obtained at www.ICGtesting.com
Printed in the USA
BVOW071346041111

275310BV00001B/1/P